St. Mary's H. S. Library
South Amboy, N. J.

crime

WORLD WAR II
HOME REPAIR AND IMPROVEMENT
THE TIME-LIFE LIBRARY OF BOATING
HUMAN BEHAVIOR
THE ART OF SEWING
THE OLD WEST
THE EMERGENCE OF MAN
THE AMERICAN WILDERNESS
THE TIME-LIFE ENCYCLOPEDIA OF GARDENING
LIFE LIBRARY OF PHOTOGRAPHY
THIS FABULOUS CENTURY
FOODS OF THE WORLD
TIME-LIFE LIBRARY OF AMERICA
TIME-LIFE LIBRARY OF ART
GREAT AGES OF MAN
LIFE SCIENCE LIBRARY
THE LIFE HISTORY OF THE UNITED STATES
TIME READING PROGRAM
LIFE NATURE LIBRARY
LIFE WORLD LIBRARY
FAMILY LIBRARY:
   HOW THINGS WORK IN YOUR HOME
   THE TIME-LIFE BOOK OF THE FAMILY CAR
   THE TIME-LIFE FAMILY LEGAL GUIDE
   THE TIME-LIFE BOOK OF FAMILY FINANCE

HUMAN BEHAVIOR

crime

BY VIRGINIA ADAMS
AND THE EDITORS OF TIME-LIFE BOOKS

St. Mary's H. S. Library
South Amboy, N. J.

TIME-LIFE BOOKS, NEW YORK

The Author: Virginia Adams is a text editor for TIME-LIFE BOOKS and a journalist specializing in the behavioral sciences. She is a graduate of Smith College, where she studied psychology, and a former writer of TIME's *Sexes* and *Behavior* sections.

General Consultants for Human Behavior:
Robert M. Krauss is Professor of Psychology at Columbia University. He has taught at Princeton and Harvard and was Chairman of the Psychology Department at Rutgers. He is the co-author of *Theories in Social Psychology,* formerly edited the *Journal of Experimental Social Psychology* and contributes articles to many journals on aspects of human behavior and social interaction.

Peter I. Rose, a specialist on racial and ethnic relations, is Sophia Smith Professor of Sociology and Anthropology at Smith College and is on the graduate faculty of the University of Massachusetts. His books include *They and We, The Subject is Race* and *Americans from Africa.* Professor Rose has also taught at Goucher, Wesleyan, Colorado, Clark, Yale, Amherst, the University of Leicester in England, Kyoto University in Japan and Flinders University in Australia.

James W. Fernandez is Professor of Anthropology at Princeton University. His field research has concentrated on cultural change in East, West and South Africa, and the Iberian peninsula. He has been President of the Northeastern Anthropological Association and a consultant to the Foreign Service Institute. He has also taught at Dartmouth College.

Special Consultant for Crime:
Marvin E. Wolfgang is Professor of Sociology and Law and former Chairman of the Department of Sociology at the University of Pennsylvania. He is currently Director of the Center for Studies in Criminology and Criminal Law and President of the American Academy of Political and Social Science. Among the books of which he is an author or editor are *Delinquency in a Birth Cohort, Patterns in Criminal Homicide* and *Crime and Justice.*

Valuable help was given by the following departments and individuals of Time Inc.: Editorial Production, Norman Airey; Library, Benjamin Lightman; Picture Collection, Doris O'Neil; Photographic Laboratory, George Karas; TIME-LIFE News Service, Murray J. Gart; Correspondents Margot Hapgood and Dorothy Bacon (London), Ann Natanson and Deborah Sgardello (Rome), Maria Vincenza Aloisi (Paris), Elisabeth Kraemer (Bonn), S. Chang and Frank Iwama (Tokyo), Bernard Diederich (Mexico City), Mary Johnson (Stockholm), Knud Meister (Copenhagen), Bing Wong (Hong Kong).

© 1976 Time Inc. All rights reserved.
First printing.
Published simultaneously in Canada.
Library of Congress catalogue card number 76-29184.
Not to be reproduced in whole or in part without permission.

TIME-LIFE BOOKS

FOUNDER: Henry R. Luce 1898-1967

Editor-in-Chief: Hedley Donovan
Chairman of the Board: Andrew Heiskell
President: James R. Shepley
Vice Chairman: Roy E. Larsen
Corporate Editor: Ralph Graves

MANAGING EDITOR: Jerry Korn
Executive Editor: David Maness
Assistant Managing Editors:
Ezra Bowen, Martin Mann
Planning Director: Oliver E. Allen
Art Director: Sheldon Cotler
Chief of Research: Beatrice T. Dobie
Director of Photography: Melvin L. Scott
Senior Text Editors: Diana Hirsh, William Frankel
Assistant Planning Director: Carlotta Kerwin
Assistant Art Director: Arnold C. Holeywell
Assistant Chief of Research: Myra Mangan

PUBLISHER: Joan D. Manley
Associate Publisher: John D. McSweeney
General Manager: John Steven Maxwell
Assistant Publisher, North America: Carl G. Jaeger
Assistant Publisher, International: David J. Walsh
Business Manager: Peter B. Barnes
Promotion Director: Paul R. Stewart
Mail Order Sales Director: John L. Canova
Public Relations Director: Nicholas Benton

HUMAN BEHAVIOR
Editorial Staff for *Crime:*
Editor: William K. Goolrick
Text Editor: David S. Thomson
Designer: Marion Flynn
Staff Writers: Carol Clingan, Richard Cravens, Kathy Ritchell
Chief Researcher: Ann Morrison
Researchers: Gail Nussbaum, Jane Sugden, Barbara Fleming, Susan Jonas, Shirley Miller, Heidi Sanford
Editorial Assistant: Janet Hubbard

Editorial Production
Production Editor: Douglas B. Graham
Assistant Production Editor: Feliciano Madrid
Operations Manager: Gennaro C. Esposito
Quality Director: Robert L. Young
Assistant Quality Director: James J. Cox
Associate: Serafino J. Cambareri
Copy Staff: David L. Harrison (chief), Eleanore W. Karsten, Florence Keith, Celia S. Beattie
Picture Department: Dolores A. Littles, Jessy Faubert
Traffic: Carmen McLellan

Contents

1 | **A Plague of Lawlessness** 7

2 | **Controversy over Causes** 41

3 | **The Professionals** 71

4 | **White-Collar Crooks** 113

5 | **The Justice System** 137

Bibliography and Acknowledgments 170

Picture Credits 171

Index 172

A Plague of Lawlessness

1

It was a sunny springtime morning, and a young businessman was halfway through his daily jogging stint (two miles in a neighborhood park) when a second jogger approached and overtook him, brushing lightly against him as he passed. Jogger No. 1's response was reflex quick: he felt his pocket for his wallet. Not there. He sprinted after jogger No. 2. "Okay, give me the wallet," he demanded. No. 2 complied at once.

The young executive was pleased to think he had thwarted a pickpocket—but stunned when he got home to find his wallet lying on his desk, exactly where he had left it before setting out for the park. He drew the second billfold from the pocket of his running outfit, compared it with his own, and saw that the two were near duplicates. Unwittingly, he had become a thief; the second runner had yielded up his own billfold.

Fortunately the stranger's wallet contained his name and telephone number, so jogger No. 1 called and, deeply embarrassed, explained about his automatic response to being jostled. He asked the unintended victim why he had so readily handed over his wallet. It had never occurred to the stranger that he was not being robbed and he had felt certain that resistance could only invite assault.

The story is true. It may be funny. But the fact that an accidental jostling in the park is perceived to be as threatening as bullet holes in a bank (left) reveals much about crime in the world today—and the public reaction to it.

Lawbreaking is as old as law. It is a major theme of the story of Genesis and has plagued mankind over the centuries since. Footpads and highwaymen (the latter rode horses) held up English travelers of the 17th, 18th and 19th centuries so regularly that highway robbery became a capital offense. "One is forced to travel, even at noon, as if one is going to battle," Horace Walpole wrote. Nineteenth Century New York was terrorized by brawling street gangs with perhaps 30,000 members, many of them ready to kill without provocation. When a certain

Chapter 1

Monk Eastman laid open the scalp of a quiet old man drinking beer and was asked his motive, he explained, "I had forty-nine nicks in me stick, an' I wanted to make it an even fifty."

Whether such murderous perversity was more or less common in the past than it is now is impossible to prove. Yet today crime seems to be increasing rapidly all over the world. The apprehension it stirs and the spell of fascination it casts have led behavioral scientists into the study of crime in depth. They have tried to assess its extent and to understand what causes it. They have analyzed criminals and recorded their methods, explaining how white-collar and professional criminals practice their various specialties. Countless studies have examined the ways in which society responds, probing the failures and accomplishments of police, courts and prisons. And finally the experts have pressed the age-old search for ways to forestall crime before it happens. The problem is immense. But how immense no one really knows, for official records are notoriously inaccurate. There are many reasons. Classifications vary, blurring country-to-country comparisons. Much crime goes undetected, even by its victims.

The "dark figure" of unreported crime may amount to as much as 10 times the recorded total. When 10,000 Americans were asked whether anyone in their family had been the victim of a crime in the previous year, it turned out that no complaints had been filed in a third of all rape and theft cases experienced by the respondents—the victims feared reprisal, felt sorry for the criminal or believed there was nothing the police could or would do.

The police themselves manipulate crime statistics, inflating them to embarrass political opponents or to buttress pleas for funds, deflating them to indicate efficiency. In 1975, the Soviet newspaper *Izvestia* printed a letter from an anonymous policeman who charged that party officials were obsessed with minimizing the crime problem, and his department and a neighboring one were waging a battle of statistics for the purpose of presenting the best possible crime picture. As a result, the policeman said, cases of petty crime were recorded as individual offenses, while instances of serious misbehavior showed up in official figures as minor wrongdoing.

Distorted as the statistics may be, they confirm a common observation: a sharp increase in crime has terrorized most of the world. Since World War II, the crime rate appears to have risen in America, most of Europe, the Soviet Union and a few rapidly developing nations. The United States population went up 13 per cent from 1960 to 1970, but the overall crime rate went up 148 per cent. Crime statistics increased

13 per cent in France and 24 per cent in Italy between 1971 and 1973. They went up 7 per cent in Germany and 18 per cent in Great Britain between 1973 and 1974.

Crimes of violence have been on the upswing almost everywhere in the world. The United States has the dubious distinction of ranking first, with an increase of 130 per cent between 1960 and 1970. One American city, Detroit, with a population of 1.5 million, has more homicides each year than all of England and Wales, with a population of 54 million. Yet violence plagues even comparatively peaceable London, which was terrorized in the 1970s by 30-odd gangs of "bovver birds," a Cockney term for fighting girls. In groups of three or four, they roamed the city at night in search of suitable prey, often "granny bashing" a lone woman waiting for a bus or by herself in a public toilet. The bovver birds would swoop down, shrieking, to overwhelm the victim with blows—and frequently with bites—before making off with her purse. "It was like having banshees wailing in my ear," said one unfortunate victim. "They kept screaming while two of them took my arms and one jabbed my back with what felt like a knife blade. They made me kneel down with the side of my face against the pavement, and they took everything I had. Then one of them took her foot and crushed my head against the pavement."

In 1975, a French journalist wrote in *L'Express* that only five years earlier, Europeans had thought of rampant city lawlessness as a phenomenon that was exclusively American. Then the situation changed. Frenchmen began to be victimized by crimes that were new to their society: subway and street muggings, attacks on the elderly in their apartments, raids on pharmacies by drug addicts, shootings in public places and the taking of hostages to ensure criminals a safe getaway after they had engaged in acts of banditry. Only six armed bank holdups occurred in the Paris area during 1966, but there were nearly 600 in 1973 and about 10 a day during the winter of 1973-1974. Criminal acts of all kinds numbered 581,618 in 1963; a decade later the total had increased to 1,763,372.

A 1975 study of crime in Europe by John Mack found that, beginning in 1945, the German crime scene was marked "by a continuing and accelerating increase in property crimes, a steady increase in the proportion of juveniles among the convicted offenders and a conspicuous increase in violence." Terrorism was an ever-present problem in the cities. Pseudopolitical urban guerrillas, roaming the country in stolen cars, bombed newspaper offices, police stations and United States

Army facilities, supporting themselves by holding up banks. In Frankfurt, widely referred to as the German Chicago, assaults, muggings and armed robberies were rife; in many cases the crimes were committed by heroin addicts (the city had 1,500 of them) in need of money for a fix. West Berlin reported a 43 per cent rise in major crimes from 1968 to 1973. By the mid-1970s, one of every 16 residents faced the unhappy statistical prospect that he would be mugged, raped or robbed before the end of the year.

Mack put the increase in the crime rate of England, Scotland and Wales at roughly 10 per cent a year from 1955 through the late 1960s. Then it zoomed upward. The 1974 rate rose nearly 20 per cent over the previous year. In London, the increase for 1974 was 16 per cent. The number of murders increased less than 6 per cent, but rape was up 16 per cent, shoplifting 20 per cent, automobile theft 25 per cent and burglary 27 per cent.

In Italy in the years between World War II and 1975, galleries and private owners lost 44,000 works of art, 26,000 of them in the last eight

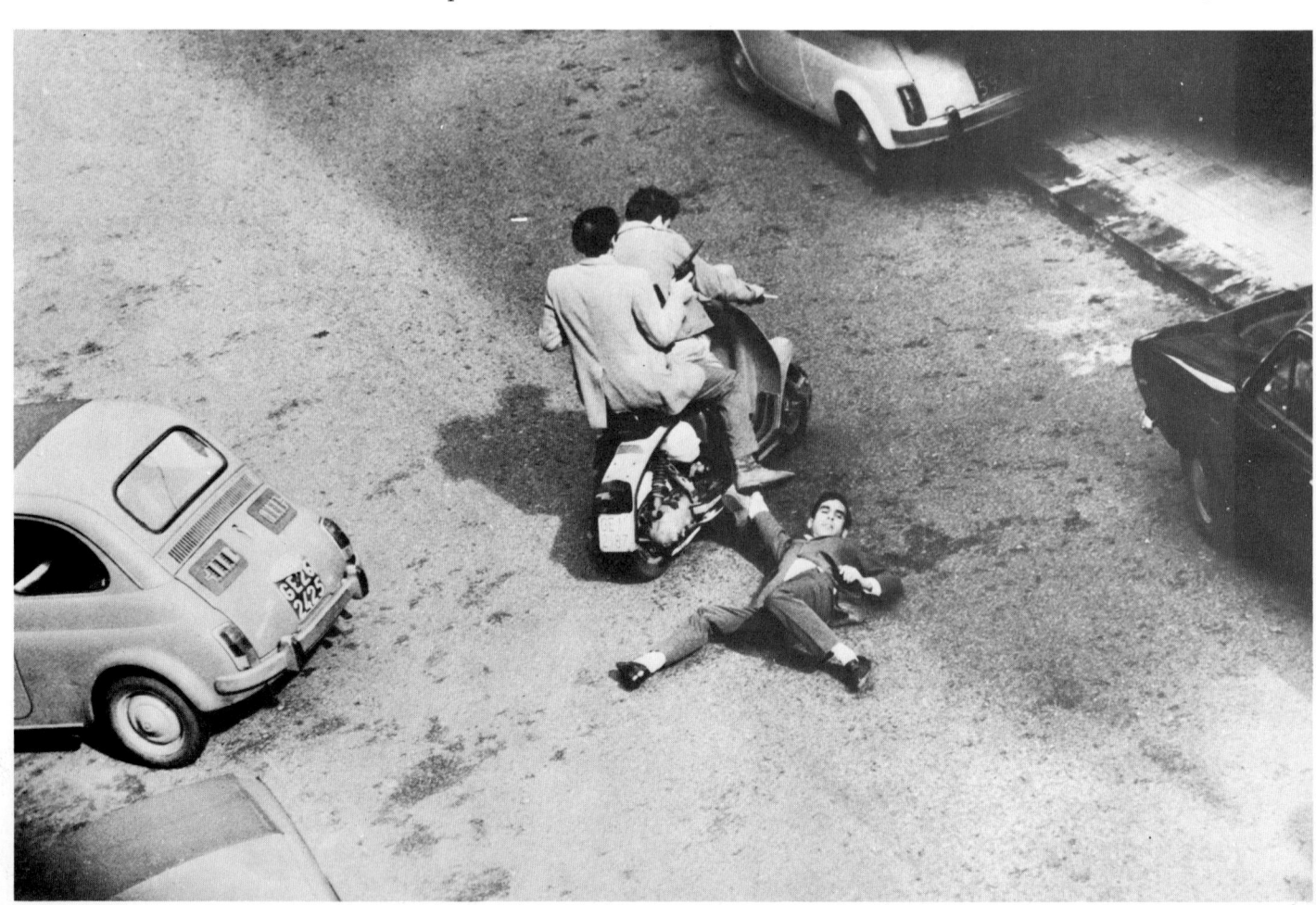

These dramatic pictures, shot by a photographer who happened to aim his camera at the street, show a 1971 murder in Italy, where violent crimes were once rare. At left, a messenger in Genoa, knocked down by bike-riding payroll thieves, bravely tries to keep them from fleeing with a satchel containing $27,200 in lire. Below, the messenger is shot to death by one of the pair. Both criminals were caught and imprisoned.

years of the period, and art theft was being called a national industry. Italy was also in the vanguard of a kidnapping wave. From 1972 to 1975, kidnappers seized 116 victims and collected ransoms totaling 60 billion lire, a sum equal to the annual income of a factory employing 3,000 workers.

Alone among industrialized nations, Japan could boast a declining rate in most crime statistics. During the decade from 1964 to 1975, arrests for violent crimes declined from 15,676 to 9,214, while arrests of juveniles dropped from 190,442 to 115,453. That the average Japanese could feel his property was safe unattended was suggested by an informal experiment conducted by a journalist. On his way to work he left a suitcase on a platform of Tokyo's Central Railway Station. Returning to check at noon, he found the suitcase still there, undisturbed by the tide of morning commuters. After the evening rush hour, too, it stood untouched.

As of the mid-'70s the Soviet Union did not appear to be doing particularly well. Westerners who visited Russia reported that it was plagued by all of the crimes familiar in Western countries, and Soviet officials acknowledged an alarming increase in "hooliganism," their term for disorderly conduct. An American who spent 1962 in and around the Moscow city court estimated that an average of two murder cases were tried each week.

The costs of crime to society are enormous. Tax evasion cost France $29 billion in 1974, Italy $5 billion. In one recent year, Italians are thought to have taken $50 billion out of their country illegally for deposit in Swiss banks; the sum is three times the amount Italy borrowed abroad to meet its bills. Shoplifting losses in West Germany came to almost $1 billion in 1974, economic crimes such as subsidy swindles and usury to $7.8 billion. And even in Japan, where crime seemed under control, the cost rose. In 1972, the Japanese lost nearly $307 million from robbery, extortion, theft, fraud and embezzlement. The Japanese system of criminal justice cost four times as much in 1971 as it had in 1961, rising to $2.3 billion.

It is not surprising that this increase in antisocial behavior has a sharp impact on the attitudes of ordinary people. In France, a poll revealed crime as the third most urgent concern, following inflation and unemployment. Two thirds of those questioned said they felt less secure than they had a few years earlier. Nearly a fifth of those polled feared that they might be physically attacked, and 44 per cent worried about theft and other property crimes. In the community of Pierre-Bénite, a suburb of Lyon, armed merchants patrolled their neighborhoods at

Chapter 1

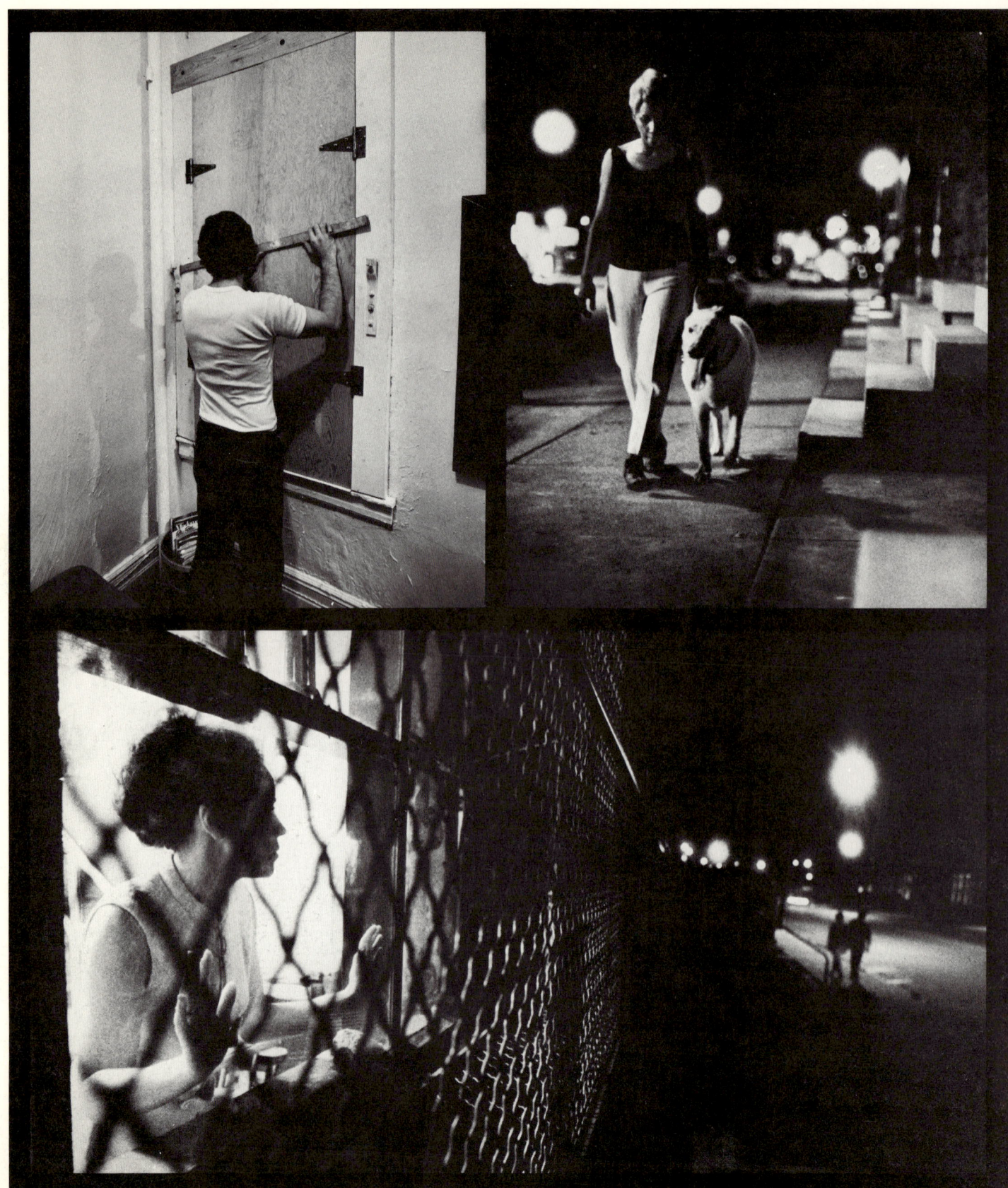

Fear of crime is so pervasive in some parts of the United States that apartment dwellers barricade themselves, nocturnal strollers walk with

12

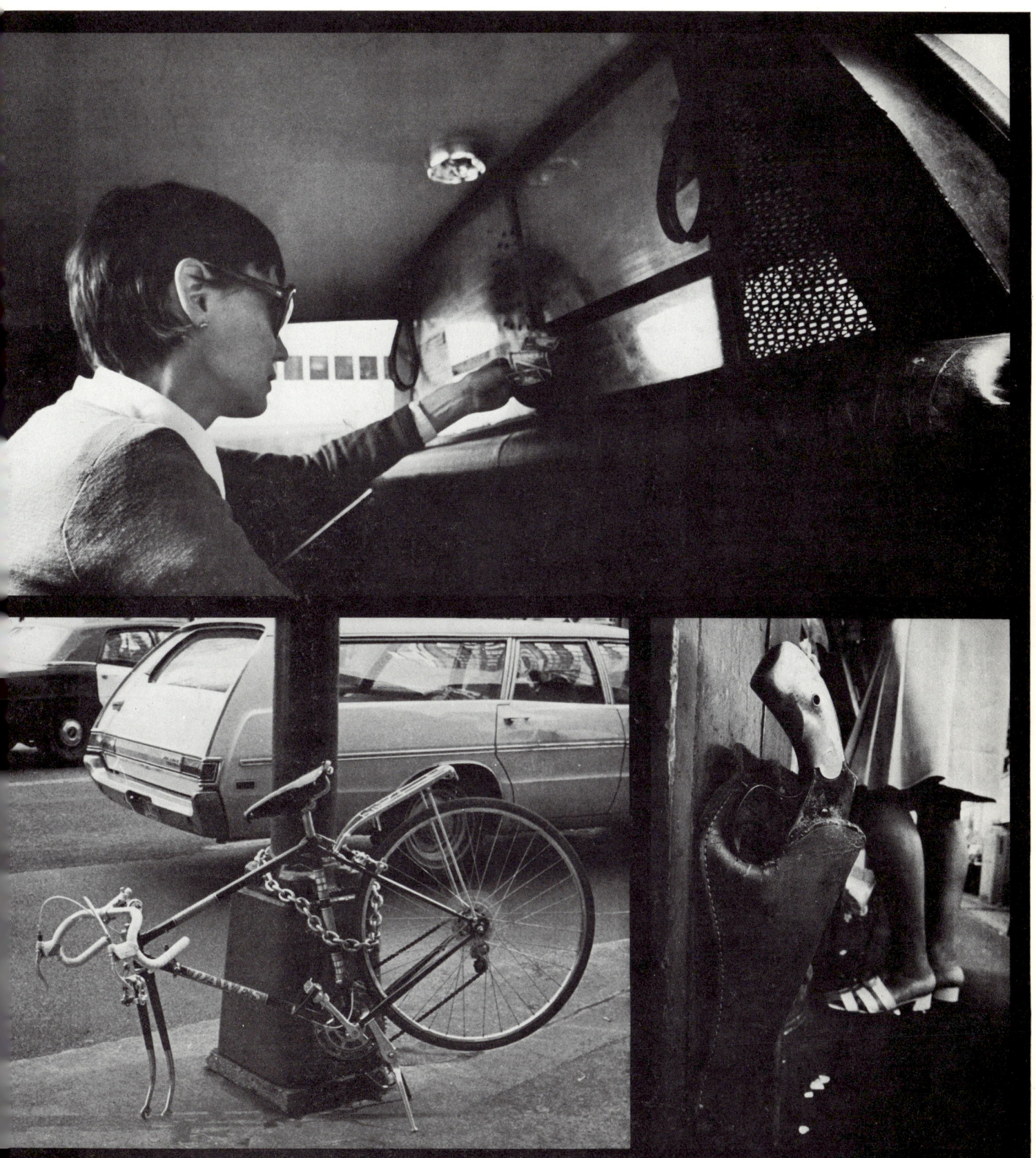
guard dogs, cab drivers seal off passengers behind bulletproof shields, cyclists dismantle and chain bikes, and clerks keep guns under counters.

Chapter 1

night. The town prefect ordered that they leave their weapons at home, but their fear of crime kept the vigilantes walking their self-assigned beats nonetheless.

In West Germany, as in most modern countries, the business of supplying canine and human guards was prospering. In Italy, guards trained in karate and licensed to carry guns were in heavy demand to protect the rich against an unprecedented wave of kidnappings. Film star Sophia Loren even moved with her children from Rome to Paris to lessen the risk of abduction. Sales of electronic burglar alarms soared everywhere in Italy. Many front doors were studded with four or five locks and further secured with four-inch-wide vertical steel plates to prevent thieves from prying their way inside. Before going off on long trips, some Italians took the precaution of pawning valuables to keep them safe. Opera first nights became dull affairs as women tried to avoid a look of affluence. Some operagoers wore gloves to cover their rings, while others, en route, tried to avoid attention by hitching up long gowns with a belt.

In 1966 Americans considered it the second most worrisome domestic problem (only race relations was thought to be a worse problem). Of Boston and Chicago residents surveyed, 43 per cent said that fear of crime kept them off the streets at night, 35 per cent said they dared not speak to strangers, and 20 per cent said they would like to move to a safer neighborhood.

Such anxiety affected rich and poor alike. In numerous cities around the world, middle-class children worried—rightly so, as experience proved—that they too might fall victim to crime. City parents frequently found themselves scouting the safest routes for their youngsters to walk to school. Sometimes they instructed their children to carry a modest amount of cash in a pocket to appease potential muggers while hiding larger sums in their shoes, and they often worried about the effect on their offsprings' personalities of counseling them not to fight for their property but to give it up prudently to anyone who accosted them.

Yet for all this fear of crime, people also find it alluring. Murder has always been a major theme in serious literature; Shakespeare wrote more than 60 murders into his plays. Detective fiction remains a genre of astonishing popularity. When Agatha Christie decided that her dapper detective Hercule Poirot had lived sufficiently long and well (he had gotten his man in 37 murder cases), major newspapers in London and New York treated his fictional death as front-page news and honored him with long obituaries.

Films as well as books celebrate the heroes of crime on both sides of the law. The French movie *Fear over the City* starred Jean-Paul Belmondo as an estimable crime fighter. The American movie *Bonnie and Clyde* romanticized a real-life pair of criminals who have been described as "about as lovable as Ilse Koch and Martin Bormann." Yet another proof of crime's power to fascinate was the smashing success, the world over, of the American film *The Godfather*; audiences everywhere made clear their approval when a young Mafia figure outwitted a rival and gunned him down over dinner.

Real lawbreaking is at least equally titillating. Gory crimes are savored, clever ones appreciated. The Great Train Robbery, the 1963 caper in which 15 well-drilled men held up a Glasgow-to-London mail train and made off with some $8 million, was the world's most lucrative robbery. It drew editorial admiration from the Sydney *Daily Telegraph*: "It proves that the homeland of Dick Turpin and Charlie Peace is not decadent. Britons may not admit that they are proud, but in private many are thinking, 'For they are jolly good felons.'"

Sociologist Gresham Sykes stated that crime was "inherently interesting . . . a basic part of the human drama. There is the mystery of the criminal act itself," he wrote, "and the ritualized conflict of the courtroom, where the innocent are separated from the guilty. There is the timeless excitement of the chase—the pursuit and capture of the man outside the law. And there is the fascination of the prison, where walls not only shut in the criminal, the contaminated man, but also shut out the public." Psychoanalyst Karl Menninger explained this inherent interest: "Society *wants* crime, *needs* crime." He added, "We need criminals to identify ourselves with, to secretly envy and to stoutly punish. Criminals represent our alter egos—our 'bad' selves—rejected and projected. They do for us the forbidden, illegal things we *wish* to do and, like the scapegoats of old, they bear the burdens of our displaced guilt and punishment."

Ambivalence toward crime may be one reason it is difficult to define. "Almost all actions of which mankind is capable have, at some time, at some place, been defined as criminal," Leslie Wilkins pointed out; "and almost all acts now defined as criminal have, at some time, at some place, been socially approved by the culture and hence not proscribed by the law." Very few acts have been defined as criminal by all societies in all eras. "Only disloyalty to the group, such as treason, and incest within the immediate family, approach the status of universal crimes," according to criminologist R. A. Laud Humphreys; some might add to this list the wanton murder of friends.

Chapter 1

While all eyes are on the matador being carried from Mexico City's bull ring in 1950, a youthful pickpocket extracts a wallet (lower left) with professional guile. No one noticed, not even the policeman nearby or the photographer, who caught the action by chance.

Most modern societies apply the criminal label not only to these few acts but also to a long list of deviant behavior that ranges from felonious assault to smoking in an elevator. Such legally created crimes break down into three groups: crimes "against the person," that is, those that cause bodily harm; crimes against property, chiefly theft; and the so-called victimless crimes that society creates when it attempts to legislate morality.

These classifications embrace a wide range of human behavior. Crimes against the person include the slugfest between two toughs in a waterfront bar as well as the 15 murders committed by the 19th Century Irishman William Burke. Burke lured travelers to a dingy boardinghouse, got them drunk, suffocated them, stowed their bodies in an old tea chest and carted them off to No. 10 Surgeons Square in Edinburgh, where anatomist Robert Knox bought them for eight to 14 pounds apiece to use in teaching and research. Property crimes run the gamut from the professional theft of cars picked to match the needs of customers ordering them in advance to the art forgeries of the 20th Century Dutch painter Hans van Meegeren, whose fake Vermeers passed as old masters among art experts and sold to museums and connoisseurs for a total of $1.3 million. Crimes without victims have in common the fact that they entail no specific physical or economic harm by one person to another. Instead, an individual performs some action disapproved of by society. The narcotics dealer provides the addict with the drugs he craves, and the addict uses the drug—each engaging in an activity that is illegal in many places.

Whether behavior is deemed a crime, and how severely it is condemned, varies from culture to culture and depends on time, place, circumstances, political system, economic and social conditions, and the prevailing moral climate.

Even the act of killing a human being has never been universally censured as crime. Beginning about 700 B.C. the *patria potestas*, or parental authority, gave Roman fathers the right to sacrifice, devour or otherwise kill their own children. Happily, very few parents availed themselves of their prerogative, although Seneca and other philosophers endorsed it. The law of ancient Sparta required parents to produce their newborn child for inspection by a council of elders; if the judges ruled the baby weak or deformed they ordered it thrown from the summit of Mount Taggetus into Apotheta, a canyon far below. In ancient Papua and in Cochin China, infanticide was a community-approved method of limiting family size.

Many preliterate societies—as well as some more modern ones—con-

Chapter 1

18

When the photograph at left was made in 1932, the brazen solicitation of this streetwalker in Paris was legal—when confined to stipulated places and hours. But attitudes toward behavior like prostitution constantly shift, and French authorities later outlawed streetwalking.

sidered killing the right and proper way for an individual to avenge a wrong that had been done him. Until the French penal code became law in Algeria, tradition required that the father or brother of an adulterous wife kill her "to cleanse by her blood the honor of her relatives." And a husband whose wife had cuckolded him had much the same license under "unwritten law" in the United States well into the 20th Century. Theft also varies in definition and importance. Stealing a horse carries a minor penalty today in most parts of the world, but during the American frontier days it was a capital offense because a horse could be vital to a settler's well-being.

In the Soviet Union, private enterprise itself is often looked on as robbery from the state. A defendant was alleged to have bought rugs in Moscow stores and resold them in the city of Frunze for twice the state-set price. In the West, he would have been considered enterprising. In the Soviet Union, he was indicted for embezzlement, bribery, theft of the people's wealth, corruption of socialist mores and disruption of the distribution plan for rugs. The outcome of his case never became known in the West, but before the trial the defendant's lawyer predicted that the state would confiscate his client's property and ship him off to a labor colony for 15 years. If that is all that happened to him, he was lucky: between 1964 and 1968, nearly 200 Soviet citizens were sentenced to death for economic crimes.

Victimless crimes are particularly subject to variability. Every modern society has at some point in its history imposed criminal sanctions for conduct it considers immoral, but in no country but America, sociologist Daniel Bell wrote, have there been "such spectacular attempts to curb human appetites and brand them as illicit, and nowhere else with such glaring failures."

Prohibition, America's attempt to keep people from drinking, was a fiasco to end all fiascoes. At least one store sold bricks of grape concentrate, along with jugs and other equipment, and provided detailed "warnings" that actually told how to convert the concentrate into illicit strong drink. "You dissolve the brick in a gallon of water," a demonstrator explained to customers. "Do not place the liquid in this jug and put it away in the cupboard for 21 days, because then it would turn into wine. Do not stop the bottle with this cork containing this patented red rubber siphon hose, because that is necessary only when fermentation is going on. Do not put the end of the tube into a glass of water, because that helps to make the fermenting liquor tasty and potable."

Within a year of the enactment of Prohibition, the one-gallon still had become a commonplace home utensil. One versifier observed:

Breaking the cycle of violence

Experts call it the least reported crime. It persists from generation to generation, affecting victims in every race and class. Most victims know no escape.

This crime is wife-beating. Since 1971, London's Chiswick Women's Aid Center has been taking in women who claim they had been battered, giving them and their children sanctuary and help. Because the Center turns no one away, it is always overcrowded. But the very bustle gives the women, accustomed to confusion in their lives, an acceptable transition to the calm of one of the Center's 21 community homes, where they go when healed enough to construct a new, peaceful life for themselves and their children.

Residents and leaders at the Chiswick Center listen attentively during a daily counseling session. Since the staff is small, most help comes from residents.

A mother tucks her child into bed with a kiss. Many of the children are also battered and, except for the Center, might grow up doing violence to their own youngsters in turn: half of their fathers had been abused by their parents.

During an art class, a play-group leader pours cold drinks for his charges. The only males in the community, the leaders are visible evidence to the women and children that men can be gentle.

*Mother's in the kitchen
Washing out the jugs;
Sister's in the pantry
Bottling the suds;
Father's in the cellar
Mixing up the hops;
Johnny's on the front porch
Watching for the cops.*

For those who enjoyed the sociability of public drinking, there were speak-easies, supposedly clandestine drinking establishments, everywhere. In New York alone there were at least 32,000, which was more than twice the number of legal drinking places before Prohibition. One street boasted so many that a woman whose house stood between two of them was forced to put up a sign that read: "This is a private residence. Do not ring."

The police did stage occasional raids, and many a bar was so ingeniously constructed that no evidence of illegal activity could be found. Recalled Charlie Berns, the proprietor of one renowned speak-easy, "We had this engineer we trusted, and he installed a series of contraptions for us that worked on different mechanical or electrical impulses. For example, the shelves behind the bar rested on tongue blocks. In case of a raid the bartender could press a button that released the blocks, letting the shelves fall backward and dropping the bottles down a chute. As they fell, they hit against angle irons projecting from the sides of the chute and smashed. At the bottom were rocks and a pile of sand through which the liquor seeped, leaving not a drop of evidence. In addition, when the button was pressed, an alarm bell went off, warning everybody to drink up fast."

Most laws intended to compel morality do not fail quite so grandly as Prohibition did, but they do not succeed very well either. This consideration, as much as a general easing of moral strictures, has promoted a trend toward decriminalization. By the 1970s, most modern countries were lifting or at least softening legal bans on conduct that inflicted no specific harm on people or property, even though many citizens might disapprove of such behavior.

Japan still had an abortion statute on the books at the beginning of 1976, but police almost never tried to enforce it. In Italy, women waged a vigorous campaign to legalize abortion on demand; in the United States the Supreme Court struck down most state laws banning abortions in early pregnancy.

Drug-related behavior provides yet another example of victimless crimes that may be on the way out. Of course, using certain drugs for pleasure has always been acceptable in certain cultures, depending on the drug and the culture. Alcohol is legal outside the Muslim world. The use of opiates has not been a crime in Italy and several other countries. With the exception of Japan, no nation has found that harsh drug laws prove very effective. Only half jokingly, Gilbert Geis remarked that it would make more sense to outlaw obesity than it would narcotics. Overweight "is more dangerous than heroin," and, he said, "uses up food." More and more, ordinary men and women seemed to be learning the lessons that criminologists had long been trying to teach. Statutes creating victimless crimes, the experts say, are so hard to enforce they foster cynicism about the law in general. They are often invoked against the poor and not the rich. They give rise to secondary crimes, dissipating police resources that might be devoted to combating truly dangerous behavior.

The chameleon nature of crime applies to the criminal as well. It is impossible to draw a portrait of the typical criminal because he simply does not exist; the people who commit crimes vary in characteristics and background just as the behavior considered criminal varies. It is possible to make a few generalizations: most criminals, it turns out, are young and male. And it is possible to dispel a few popular myths. Social ills such as poverty may breed crime—at least it is clear that poor people are more likely to go to jail than rich ones—but lawbreaking is just as clearly not limited to the underprivileged. Nor, despite many attempts through the years, has convincing evidence been found of physical characteristics, external or internal, that identify a tendency toward criminal behavior.

While the genes may not lead an individual into crime, youth may. Age is so important that one sociologist predicted muggings would decrease in New York City not because of any police action but simply because the population was growing older. The statistics are plain. In the United States juveniles account for far more than their share of arrests and for a substantial percentage of violent crimes. In America, 15 is the peak age of crimes of violence. Forty-five per cent of Americans arrested for street crimes are under 18 (the percentage of the population below that age is 32). Sociologist Marvin Wolfgang of the University of Pennsylvania studied 10,000 boys who were born in 1945 and had lived in Philadelphia between the ages of 10 and 18. Of these, 35 per cent had acquired a police record by the time they were 18. Of this group, 46 per cent never committed another crime, or at least were

Chapter 1

24

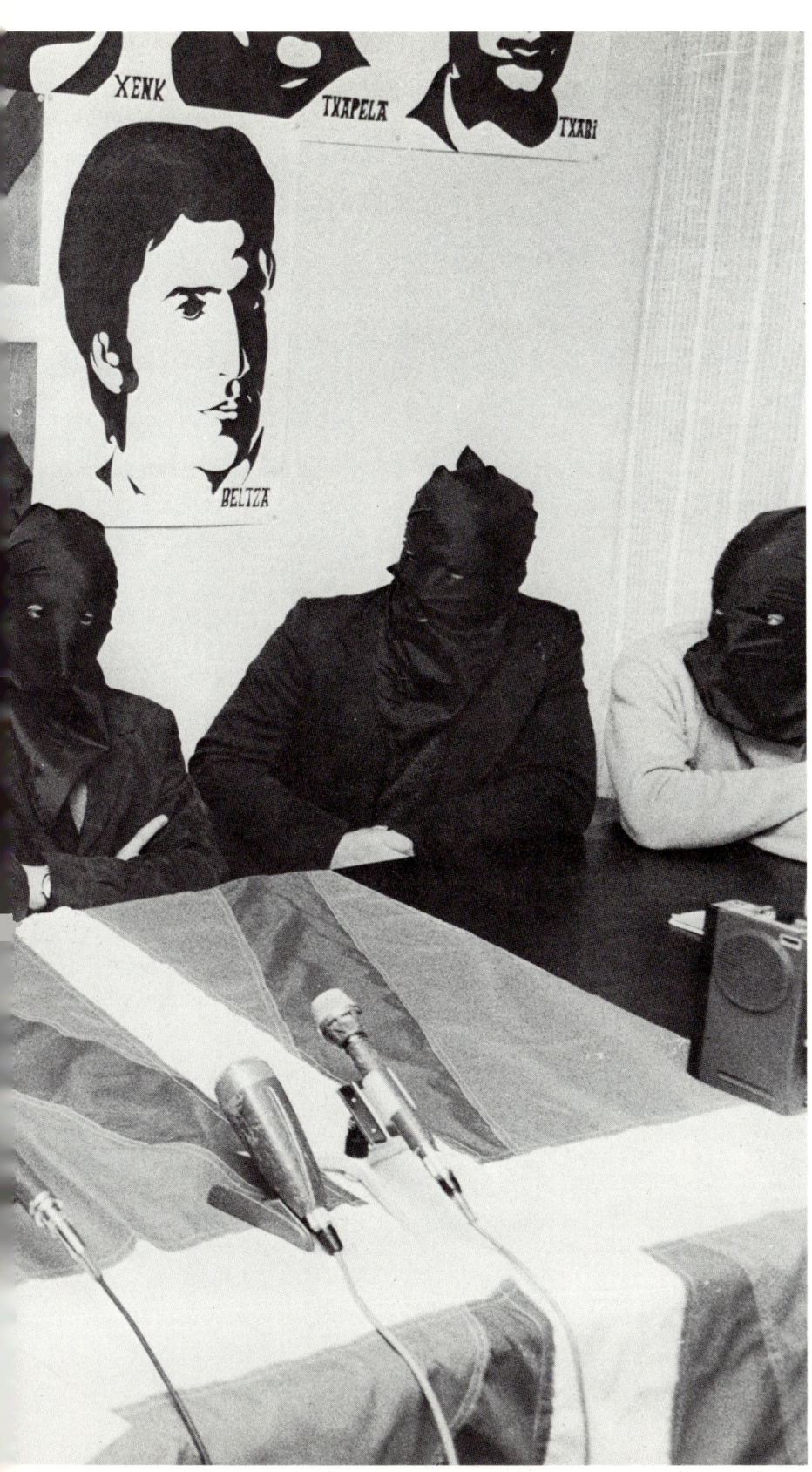

Basque terrorists hold a press conference in 1973 after killing the Spanish premier in their fight for independence from Spain. Savage political crimes, a mounting problem during the 1960s and '70s, proved almost impossible to control, partly because the terrorists exhibited no personal fear. "To this kind of mentality," observed psychiatrist David Hubbard, "death is not the ultimate punishment but the ultimate reward."

never arrested again, and another 35 per cent gave up crime after their second arrest. They stopped breaking the law as they grew older. But there was a hard core of repeaters who were the real problem. In the end, 627 of the original 3,475 wound up as chronic offenders.

Trevor Gibbens, a University of London psychiatrist who studied young offenders such as the bovver birds, noted, "Many of their attacks are for pure game, mostly done on the spur of the moment." Most of the girls were poor and underprivileged—but not all. One bovver bird worked as secretary to a company director, lived in her father's costly house, and had a car and a horse of her own.

Most criminals are not female but male. Edwin Schur reports that he often tells his sociology students, "Picture in your mind a typical criminal"; when he does, he says, the vast majority think of a man. The stereotype is reasonably accurate. Yet many criminals are women, and their number is increasing—a trend attributed by many to the general equalization of male and female behavior.

In the United States, the number of boys under the age of 18 who were arrested for serious offenses went up about 80 per cent between 1960 and 1972; for women, the increase was more than 306 per cent. In England, Sir Leon Radzinowicz, professor of criminology at Cambridge University, said in 1973 that although women traditionally accounted for only one eighth of the criminal population, they appeared to be rapidly closing the gap between men and themselves. Radzinowicz reported that when women did men's jobs during World War II, their crime rate went up, and that when men came home from the War and took back their old jobs, the female crime rate dropped to its normal level. "This is one of criminology's few laws," he explained. "Any member of society who starts to take an increasing role in the economic and social life of that society will be more exposed to crime and will have more opportunities and therefore will become more vulnerable and more prone to criminal risk."

While it may be true that much crime can be traced to young males, other generalizations turn out to be false. Lawlessness is not a specialty of the lower classes, or of particular ethnic groups or genetic types.

It appears to be an accident of time and place that in the United States organized crime—the big business of the Mafia syndicates—is dominated by men of Italian descent. They make up only a tiny fraction of the total population of hardworking, perfectly honest Italian-Americans. Other countries have their own criminal organizations.

The Dacoits of the Chambal Valley near New Delhi, India, have made violence a way of life and almost a proud tradition; in a single year, they were responsible for 285 murders, 352 kidnappings and 213 robberies. One Dacoit, queried about how many policemen he had killed, replied: "If I asked you how many pieces of bread you've eaten in the past two months, could you tell me?"

In Japan the crime syndicates are the *boryokudan* (violence organizations), whose members are called *yakuza*, or good-for-nothings. In 1973, the country had 2,900 *boryokudan* with a membership of 124,000. The largest of the syndicates was *Yamaguchi-gumi*, which means Yamaguchi's team and was named for the organization's first boss, Harukichi Yamaguchi. *Yamaguchi-gumi* had 10,000 members, earned $100 million a year from illicit gambling operations alone, and controlled 50 or more corporations, including restaurants, bars, trucking companies and talent agencies.

If no ethnic group has a monopoly on crime, neither does any social class. The best people break the law. A President of the United States was deposed because he condoned illegal activities, and scandals in the 1970s exposed wrongdoing at the highest levels of government in Japan and Europe. Such ostensibly respectable people who violate trust placed in them—the bank officer who embezzles depositors' funds, the executive who cheats customers by collusion, the businessman who gets ahead by bribery—are white-collar criminals. In the opinion of some authorities, they do more harm to society than do the muggers and thieves who arouse so much public indignation.

It seems that anyone could be a criminal. Most authorities agree that anyone could be. But some are more likely to break the law than others. And social scientists continue the centuries-old attempt to find out why —to identify the causes of crime, whether they lie within the individual or around him in his culture.

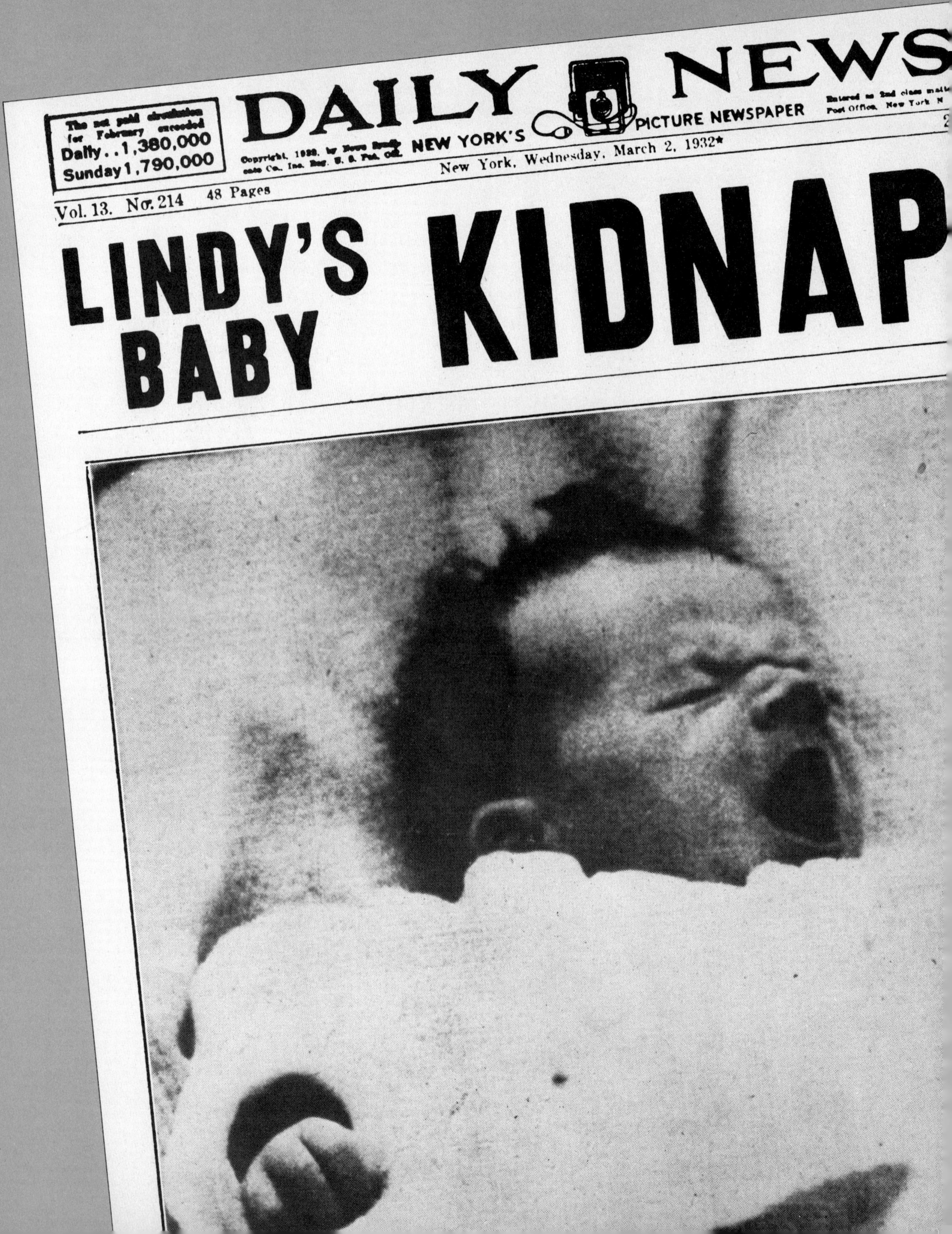

The net paid circulation for February exceeded
Daily..1,380,000
Sunday 1,790,000

DAILY NEWS

NEW YORK'S PICTURE NEWSPAPER

Copyright, 1932, by News Syndicate Co., Inc. Reg. U. S. Pat. Off.

Entered as 2nd class matte
Post Office, New York N

New York, Wednesday, March 2, 1932★

Vol. 13. No. 214 48 Pages

LINDY'S BABY KIDNAP

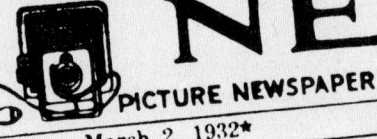

The crime of the century

In happier days, Charles and Anne Lindbergh pause beside their plane after a joint flight. Mrs. Lindbergh won acclaim for taking up flying with Lindy.

On March 2, 1932, newspaper headlines across the world screamed that the impossible, the unimaginable had happened. Charles Augustus Lindbergh Jr., 20-month-old son of the famed aviator, the Lone Eagle, had been kidnapped.

In this crime, perhaps the most notable and poignant of the century, the role of the public was remarkable. People are always fascinated by crime, for reasons that have inspired much psychoanalytical speculation *(page 39)*, but the involvement of the general population in the Lindbergh kidnapping exceeded anything known before. Everyone had seen pictures of the golden-haired child, called by the New York *Daily News* "the most famous baby in the world." To the horror that accompanies any kidnapping was added an extra dimension—"an intense feeling of individual and personal affront," noted a psychiatrist, "at this crime against the adored citizen of the world."

For more than four years, during the search for the baby, the hunt for his killer, the stages of the trial and finally the execution of the convicted murderer, Bruno Richard Hauptmann, on April 3, 1936, every development was chronicled in minute detail by the press. Millions became armchair detectives. Thousands of spectators began to gather at the Lindbergh home every day —the vanguard of an army of amateur detectives and curiosity seekers who actively participated in the long drama. Such gawking became so unbearable that Colonel and Mrs. Lindbergh, who had built an out-of-the-way house in an ardent desire for privacy, left the United States in 1935 to live in England.

Police Fail in Search for Lindbe[rgh]

John Hughes Curtis fraudulently convinced Lindbergh he knew the kidnap gang.

Cashing in on a tragedy

In the days following the kidnapping of Charles Lindbergh Jr., even the staid *New York Times*—which usually downplays crime—began to run a front-page box entitled "The Kidnapping Situation." Such press coverage helped incite readers to stick their oars into the case, splashing up false clues, hampering the police and sometimes revealing an evil tendency in human nature seldom seen so starkly. Phony ransom notes poured into the Lindbergh house. False sightings of the baby were reported daily; many were genuine attempts to help but others were purely malicious. But the most vicious interventions were deliberate frauds of swindlers—such as the financially harassed shipbuilder above—who tried to cash in on the readiness of the unhappy family to pay ransom for the return of their baby.

RK TIMES, FRIDAY, MARCH 4, 1932.

gh Kidnappers, Tracing Many False Clue
LINDBERGH CASE AND NEW PICTURES OF THE MISSING CHILD.

MYRIAD OF CLUES PROVE FALSE HE

Police Spend a Day of Int
Activity and Admit Failur
Kidnapping Hunt.

EVERY LEAD IS RUN D

Lindbergh Sends for Detective
an Old Friend—New Jersey
Calls on Mulrooney.

The New York police, wor
cooperation with the New
authorities in the hunt for th
bergh baby and his captor
another day of intense activ
ing down a multitude of c
admitted last night that t
found no definite informatio
case in this city.
Police headquarters was
with hundreds of letters
cards and telephone messa
individuals giving what th
were clues or giving sugges
the search. Some of th
plausible, but others were
evitable crank messages
conspicuously publicized
ways elicits.
One of the tips seemed
that Commissioner Mulro
self joined in running it
worked at it until 2 o'clo
day morning. At that h
peared to have collapsed
Commissioner still had
working on it yesterday.
to state its nature.
"Every suggestion, ever
reaches us, no matter ho
appears, is being run do
missioner Mulrooney expl
are not passing up any
get information in this c

Many False Lea

New York City, like a s
big centres yesterday, h
of reports of strangely
sons in automobiles and
the new radio alarm s,
ing license numbers and
to patroling police autor
by one they were chec
regretfully eliminated
Commissioner Mulroo
in his office yesterday
Chief Inspector Daniel
sey City and at noon w
a young woman whos
and identity were for
secret. She was Miss
Walker, employe in a r
ice cream parlor at P
J., eight miles from
estate. Miss Walker'
shielded for a while
who called her "Miss
was brought to New
Headquarters by New
tives and for a time it
she might have seen t
Her clue, however,

One of 2,000 crank ransom notes received by the Lindberghs in a single day, this postcard mailed in Auburn, New York, like all the others, sent the police on a wild-goose chase.

A week after the kidnapping, some of the army of reporters and photographers who kept newspapers filled with sensational accounts grab a makeshift lunch under a bridge near the Lindbergh home.

John F. Condon, code-named Jafsie after his initials, turned over $50,000 to a man who called himself John—but proved his identity to Jafsie with symbols used on the ransom demand, two overlapping circles and three square holes.

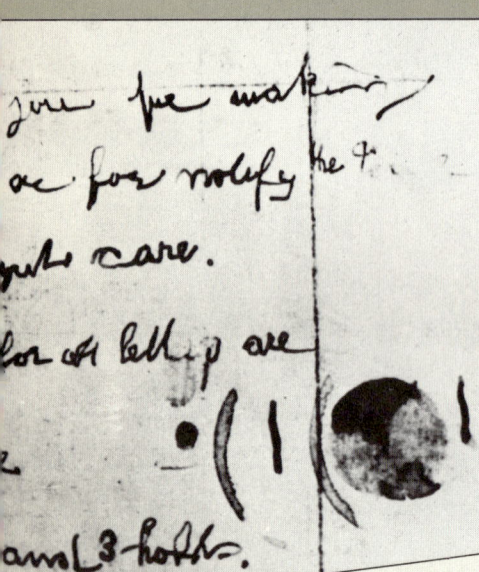

Crucial lead from a go-between

While public involvement disrupted investigation and violated tenets of decent behavior, it also started the case toward its denouement. A note demanding a ransom of $50,000 *(left)* had been found, and Lindbergh promptly offered to pay through two underworld intermediaries. But the person who actually made contact with the kidnapper was a total stranger motivated perhaps by compassion, or a desire for publicity.

Dr. John F. Condon, a 72-year-old retired educator, wrote a letter to a newspaper, offering to act as a confidential go-between. To his and everyone else's surprise, the kidnapper accepted; he received a response bearing the kidnapper's secret identification. Condon turned over the ransom money in a cemetery, and was given directions to the baby. The child was not there. Seventy-two days later, his body was found —accidentally. He had been dead since shortly after the abduction.

Armed with torches, neighbors conduct a late-night search of the woods around the Lindbergh home for traces of the baby, near the spot where a truck driver later happened on the body. The public made the tragedy a circus; popcorn vendors set up at the grave, and the truck driver was displayed at an amusement park.

A telltale trail of ransom money

In defiance of the kidnapper's instructions, the serial numbers on the ransom currency had been recorded. Whenever it was spent, the ransom money was quickly detected by bank officials in New York City. With colored pins, police plotted on a map the areas where it was most often passed, and finally narrowed the apparent home ground of the kidnapper to two sections, one in Manhattan and one in the Bronx. Now the numbers were published and ordinary citizens were invited to do what they had been doing all along uninvited: catch the criminal. Two of them did.

Two years after the kidnapping two service-station attendants made a note of the license number of a car driven by a man who paid for fuel with the telltale currency. The police quickly traced the automobile to a carpenter named Bruno Richard Hauptmann, and arrested him for murder.

John Lyons and Walter Lyle spotted the bill that led to Hauptmann.

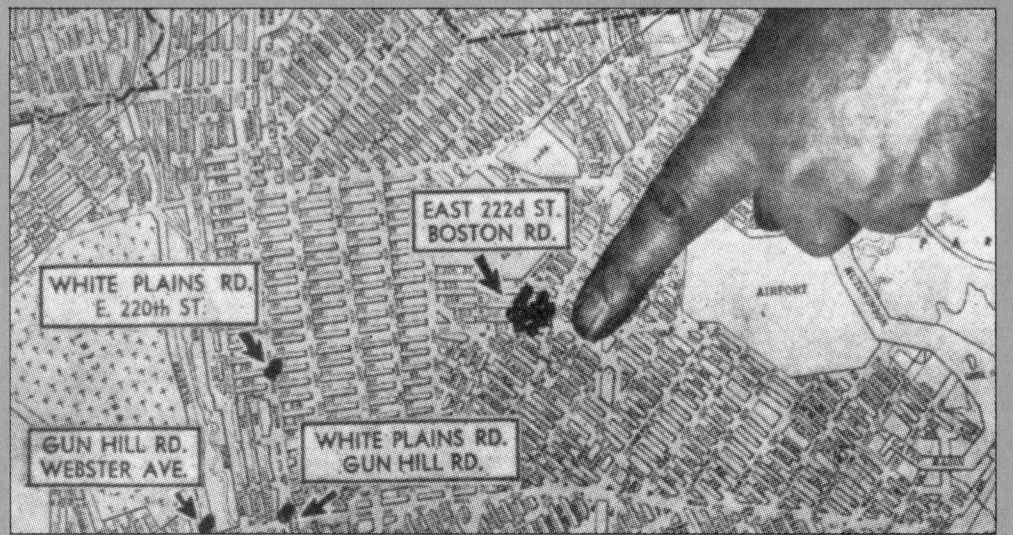

As predicted, kidnapper Hauptmann lived in the area where most of the ransom money was spent.

Spectators mill around near Hauptmann's home, where policemen found $13,750 of the ransom money in the garage.

NING, SEPTEMBER 22, 1934.

KNIVES FLY IN STRIKE

Vegetable Fields Fight Scene

Two Officers Hurt in Clash With Filipino Pickets in Salinas Valley

Further Bloodshed Feared as Lettuce and Artichoke Workers Defiant

Lindbergh Kidnaping Suspect Linked With Ladder in Crime

First Picture of Suspect

NEW CLEWS DISCLOSED

Net Tightening on Hauptmann

District Attorney in Bronx Reports Iron-clad Case After Disclosures

New Jersey Begins Move to Lay Murder Charge Against Prisoner

NEW YORK, Sept. 22.

In the building where Hauptmann is on trial, souvenir hawkers do a brisk trade in miniatures of the ladder he used to reach the nursery window. Some purchasers hung the gewgaws around their necks or pinned them to their coats.

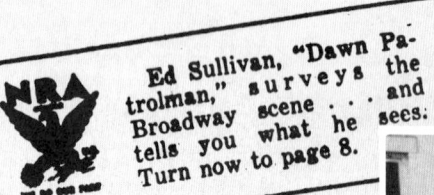

The Washing[ton]

WEDNESDAY

Ed Sullivan, "Dawn Patrolman," surveys the Broadway scene... and tells you what he sees; Turn now to page 8.

NO. 21,384

ENTERED AS POSTOFFICE.

Wirep[hoto]

Hauptmann Goes on Trial For His Life In N. J. Today

Carpenter Faces Bar of Justice 30 Months After Crime.

Outcome to Hinge Upon His Alibi

Prisoner Faces Arrest by New York Should Jury Free Him.

Flemington, N. J., Jan. 1 (U.P.)—Thirty weary months after the Lindbergh baby was kidnaped and killed, the State of New Jersey brings a prisoner to the bar of justice tomorrow to try him for the crime.

By the opinions of 12 persons the jury box in the court of oyer and terminer, Bruno Richa[rd] Hauptmann will live or die. N[ew] Jersey law dictates that he eit[her] must perish in the electric ch[air] or go back, a free man, into a w[orld] there is scarcely a fire[side his name...

36

A trial in a circus setting

The trial of Bruno Richard Hauptmann for the abduction and murder of the Lindbergh infant, conducted before a local judge and a jury of ordinary residents in an old-fashioned country town near the family estate, scrupulously followed the solemn procedures of law. But outside the simple courtroom—and even inside—avid public curiosity mocked the serious proceedings.

A child had been killed and a man's life was at stake, yet to many thousands the tragic event was fun, a special happening to be savored. Celebrities such as Jack Benny, Clifton Webb and Lynn Fontanne vied for seats in the courtroom—it was the place to be seen. Some 300 reporters covered the trial, supplying sensation-hungry readers with plenty of hyperbole. Novelist Edna Ferber, who acted as special correspondent for *The New York Times*, expressed the dismay of many observers: "the jammed aisles, the crowded corridors, the noise, the buzz, the idiot laughter, the revolting faces of those who are watching are an affront to civilization."

The jury leaves the courthouse through massed spectators who gathered every day in hope of getting a seat inside. Those who succeeded looted the courtroom, taking away everything they could get their hands on as mementos.

37

The crowd outside the courthouse waves and cheers on learning that Bruno Hauptmann (right, being led out of court) was found guilty of murder. A sentence of death was followed by repeated stays, forced by public doubts that he was solely responsible. But finally, on April 3, 1936, the kidnapper of Charles A. Lindbergh Jr. was executed.

Behind a mass mania

A half century later, the grotesque public behavior triggered by the Lindbergh case still raises many questions. The exaggerated curiosity and cruel actions of so many people cannot be explained solely by the enormous popularity of the protagonists. Rather, psychiatrists see a more universal and internal cause for this phenomenon and for the related preoccupation with crime in literature and drama. They believe that, hidden in the psyche, each person has criminal impulses that he controls so well that he is not even aware of them. But news of a murder or other violent crime releases these repressed feelings, allowing people to experience crime on a vicarious basis, safely and legally.

"Criminals represent our alter ego—our 'bad' selves," wrote Karl Menninger. "They do for us the forbidden, illegal things we *wish* to do and, like scapegoats of old, they bear the burdens of our displaced guilt and punishment."

Another authority, Walter Bromberg of the University of the Pacific, agreed: "The criminal acts out those impulses and fantasies which the law-abiding citizen represses and abhors." Bromberg summed up this idea in words that might have been written about the reaction to the kidnapping of Charles Lindbergh Jr. and the guilt of Bruno Richard Hauptmann: "Society loves its crime but hates its criminals."

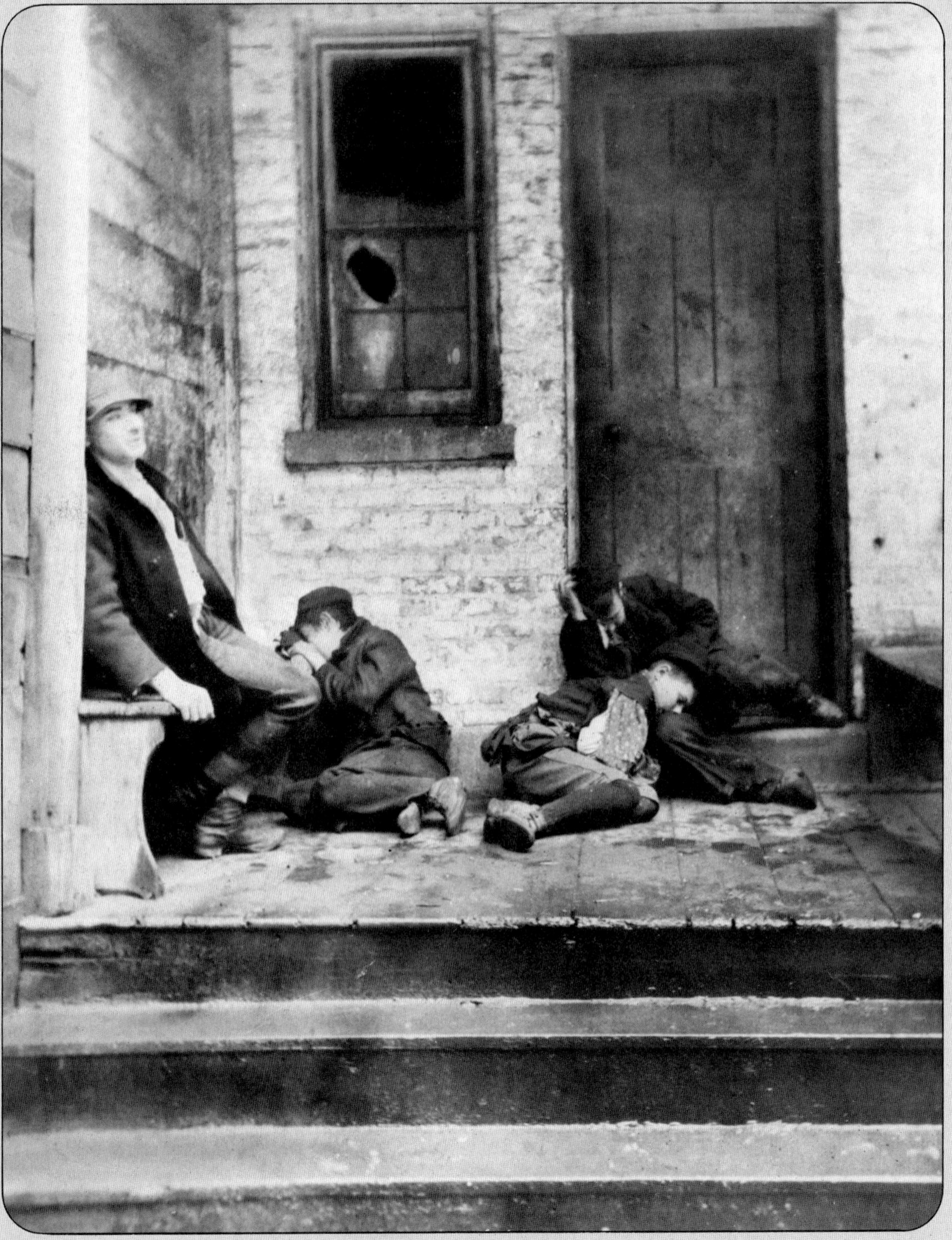

2
Controversy over Causes

"I am a liar.
"I am a thief.
"I am a murderer.
"I am a degenerate. . . .
"I am now 38 years old. Of these 38 years I have spent 22 years in jail, reform schools and prisons. In all of my lifetime I have never done any good to myself or anyone else. I am a first-class A-1 skunk. . . . I am fully aware of the fact that I am no good and that no one likes or respects me, which worries me not at all because I don't like or respect anyone else. I despise, detest and hate every human being on earth, including my own self."

This chilling statement comes from the autobiography of a criminal who murdered a score of men without suffering apparent remorse and thought up a plan for annihilating the entire human race. After studying the plan and its misanthropic creator, psychoanalyst Karl Menninger pronounced the former "by no means absurd in its conception" and the latter "possessed of superior intelligence."

Despite this criminal's bitterness and cruelty, he was able to feel lasting affection for an official who had once befriended him. He expressed an interest in ways of making the world better and believed that "it was possible for me to have lived constructively and to have been the means of much good both to myself and my fellow men if I had been properly taught and treated right in the beginning by the law." In the end, he was hanged. He ascended the gallows with cheerful readiness.

Despite its sensational features, this case raises the same question that people ask about all crime and all criminals: why? For centuries, theologians, philosophers, reformers and scientists tried to find a single explanation. In the 19th Century, slum poverty *(left)* was blamed; in the 20th, a childhood without love. Today most authorities have abandoned the attempt to isolate any one cause, recognizing that the causes are many, and difficult to separate. Anthropologist Walter Miller compared crime to cancer, in which the same set of factors produces normal cell growth in some people and abnormal growth in others.

The difficulty in fathoming the causes of crime is demonstrated by the inexplicability of lawlessness in Glasgow. Long famous for shipbuilding, the Scottish city on the River Clyde became even better known for its intractable crime problem. Why this city, in the normally law-abiding British Isles, should suffer so much from thievery, gangsterism and violence is a mystery. But suffer it does. Between 1965 and 1973, Glasgow's murder rate tripled, and by the early 1970s, 15,000 of the city's population of 862,000 belonged to rough and often violent gangs.

In the space of just one year, a young welder named William McEwan reported the occurrence of at least five crimes in or near his home. At 2 o'clock one morning, a gang broke into McEwan's apartment and looted his living room bare. Four bricks were hurled through his bedroom window on another occasion. There was a major gang fight outside his building on yet another day, and the day after that, McEwan's six-year-old daughter discovered six knives and a bayonet as she was playing in the family garden. A university student was slashed with a razor and two of his fingers were nearly severed as he stood waiting at a nearby bus stop one night, and a few days after that, a middle-aged woman was stabbed on her way home. McEwan took all this violence philosophically. He said the year was typical, and he did not consider moving, although he admitted that "you really need a dog around here."

Because McEwan's experience was not unusual, 20th Century Glasgow became a mecca for non-Glaswegian criminologists. But these outside experts have had little success in explaining Glasgow's crime. A local study panel did no better. In 1973, the group reported that there seemed to be no pattern to the city's crime, that its causes, when they could be understood at all, varied from one incident to another, and that in some parts of the city crime was "accepted as a normal form of behavior." A youth of 17 was quoted as saying, "You can be swatting someone in the face with a stick one night and the next day be talking to him on the bus." Another gang member explained, "See the feelin' in yir belly goin' into battle, it's like the feelin' ye have when Rangers are attackin' the Celtic goal. Yir heart's racin', ye feel sick—it's better'n sex."

The difficulty of explaining crime, in Glasgow and elsewhere, has not prevented the experts from trying. And some of their theories help to explain particular crimes, even though no one hypothesis seems generally applicable. Most explanations fall into one of two main categories. Theories in the first group locate the causes of crime inside the individual, and stress either biological or psychological factors. Theories in the second category place the causes of crime outside the individual, in society itself; these hypotheses are sociological.

Most biological explanations are what might be called bad-seed theories. They hold that criminals are born and not made, that a lawbreaker comes into the world with a flawed body that dooms him to a life of crime or at least predisposes him toward it. Every attempt to identify such fatal flaws has failed, but new efforts are constantly being made, often by scientists with imposing credentials.

Among the most celebrated of the early attempts to link biology to crime was that of the 19th Century Italian surgeon Cesare Lombroso. His 1876 book, *L'uomo delinquente*, or *The Criminal Man*, held that a criminal was a throwback, a vestigial survivor from primitive times. Presumably lower on the evolutionary scale than ordinary men, the law violator was said to be ruled by atavistic instincts that made him incapable of obeying modern laws.

Lombroso got the inspiration for his theory while he was doing a post mortem on the notorious brigand Vilella, a man reputedly so strong that he could scale mountains with a sheep slung over his shoulder. Lombroso's own purple prose best describes the "revelation" that came to him at the sight of Vilella's skull: "I seemed to see all of a sudden, lighted up as a vast plain under a flaming sky, the problem of the nature of the criminal—an atavistic being who reproduces in his person the ferocious instincts of primitive humanity and the inferior animals. Thus were explained anatomically the enormous jaws, high cheekbones, prominent superciliary arches, solitary lines in the palms, extreme size of the orbits, handle-shaped or sessile ears found in criminals, savages and apes, insensibility to pain, extremely acute sight, tattooing, excessive idleness, love of orgies, and the irresistible craving for evil for its own sake, the desire not only to extinguish life in the victim, but to mutilate the corpse, tear its flesh and drink its blood."

Today it seems astonishing that this nonsense could impress anyone, but Lombroso's research sounded persuasive at the time. He took a caliper and a tape measure to the bodies of Italian prisoners and soldiers, looking for what he arbitrarily judged to be "stigmata." He decided that arms beyond a certain length were excessively long and counted them as a defect. He also noted peculiarities of the eye, deviations in the size and shape of the head, and receding chins. A full 43 per cent of his criminal subjects had five or more such "anomalies," while 11 per cent of his soldiers had from one to three, and none had as many as five.

Surprisingly, the reputable English psychiatrist Havelock Ellis was

Chapter 2

44

The criminal face—fact or fancy

In 1947, to test the notion that facial characteristics distinguish criminals, LIFE ran photographs of persons convicted of serious crimes alongside posed "mug shots" of members of the professional society of detective-fiction authors, Mystery Writers of America, and challenged readers to tell them apart. Anticipating that most people would make inaccurate identifications, LIFE suggested that spotting the "dishonest" face "is a highly overrated method of criminal identification." To find out who's what, turn the page.

45

among those who made the mistake of taking Lombroso seriously. In 1913, Ellis published a book, *The Criminal*, which pursued Lombroso's fantastic ideas and carried endless photographs of criminals with such characteristics as nonexistent chins, small eyes, sneaky expressions and brutish-looking bodies.

A more skeptical Englishman of the same period, Charles Goring, decided to test Lombroso's hypothesis. Using the Italian criminologist's own standards, he compared thousands of criminals with control groups of university students and sailors and detected no important physical differences between those who broke the law and those who obeyed it. Goring came to the conclusion that "there is no such thing as an anthropological type."

Despite the evidence gathered by Goring—and dozens of careful, skeptical investigators since—theories on the innate depravity of criminals continue. One that dies hard is based on the "body type"

Who they are: nine writers, eight crooks

1 Brett Halliday wrote stories about a detective named Michael Shayne. He was married to writer Helen McCloy *(No. 6)*.
2 E. Walbridge McCully wrote the novels *Blood on Nassau's Moon* and *Death Rides a Tandem*.
3 William Manners was the editor of *Mystery Novel Classics,* a detective-story magazine, and served on the board of experts of a radio show, *Crime Quiz*.
4 Wayne Lonergan came back from World War II in 1943 and shattered his wife's skull with a candlestick. He was sentenced to a minimum of 35 years.
5 Alfred Cline, a Colorado choir singer, made a good living by marrying ladies he met at church socials. They all died suddenly, and he got 126 years.
6 Helen McCloy created the character Basil Willing, who solves crimes through extensive knowledge of psychiatry.
7 Joseph R. "Yellow Kid" Weil was an accomplished swindler who specialized in fleecing greedy bankers *(page 79)*.
8 Johnny Torrio, an Al Capone henchman who was one of Chicago's big racketeers in the 1920s, was never convicted of anything worse than income-tax evasion.
9 Winnie Ruth Judd murdered two women in 1931 and shipped their bodies to Los Angeles in a trunk. Declared insane, she was committed to an asylum.
10 Kurt Severin specialized in writing stories about crimes that took place in Latin America.
11 Lawrence Treat wrote *B as in Banshee, D as in Dead* and *V as in Victim*. He served as vice-president of Mystery Writers of America.
12 Lawrence G. Blochman wrote the book *Bombay Mail* and the movie *Quiet Please, Murder*.
13 Basil "The Owl" Banghart, machine gunner for the Chicago Touhy gang, got a 99-year sentence for kidnapping and wound up in Alcatraz.
14 Veronica Parker Johns wrote *Shady Doings* and *The Singing Widow*.
15 Manfred B. Lee collaborated with Frederic Dannay under the joint pseudonym Ellery Queen on dozens of novels and radio and TV shows.
16 Kathryn Kelly teamed up with her husband, a bank robber named "Machine Gun" Kelly, for a 1933 kidnapping; both were sentenced to life imprisonment.
17 John Fiorenza, a Manhattan upholsterer, raped and strangled writer Nancy Titterton in 1936. He was electrocuted nine months later.

classifications first developed by William Sheldon, a psychiatrist, and later applied by Eleanor and Sheldon Glueck. Mesomorphs, they said, are muscular and aggressive; endomorphs are soft, round and placid; ectomorphs are thin, fragile and introverted. After taking the body measurements of hundreds of boys whom he identified as delinquents, Sheldon made the claim that they were predominantly mesomorphic and that nondelinquents he had studied were generally endomorphic or ectomorphic. Critics who analyzed these findings said that even Sheldon's own data did not show these physical differences. Anthropologist Sherwood L. Washburn went so far as to call Sheldon's approach no more than "a new phrenology in which the bumps of the buttocks take the place of the bumps on the skull."

The most recently advanced bad-seed theory of crime derives from studies of the chromosomes that control heredity and sex. The cells of females are pairs of the X type. Those of normal males are mixed pairs, one X combined with one Y type. But some men are born with an extra Y chromosome in their genetic makeup—each cell containing one X with two Ys—and such males have been held to be especially likely to become criminals. The theory is based on surveys of a few hundred American, Australian and British prisoners. According to the researchers, the XYY syndrome turned up more often among the prison inmates than among normal men.

The XYY syndrome has been used—unsuccessfully—as a defense in at least two murder trials, the contention being that an XYY criminal should not be blamed for his behavior. One case was that of Daniel Hugon of Paris. As XYY males sometimes do, Hugon grew exceptionally tall. His six-foot-plus stature made him the butt of cruel jokes as a child and led him to quit school. Before long, he had become an alcoholic and drifter, although employers who hired him for menial jobs said he was polite and hard working. In 1965, Hugon picked up a prostitute named Marie-Louise Olivier and went with her to a shabby hotel on the Place Pigalle. Only there, when he got a good look at her, did he see that she was anything but young. In fact, she was 62. Hugon was repelled, declined to go to bed with her, and spent the night pacing the floor while Marie-Louise slept. In the morning, she insisted that he pay her 50 francs. It was all the money he had, but Hugon handed it over —and then strangled her.

In court, the respected geneticist Jerome Lejeune advanced the controversial argument that although "the born criminal does not exist," people with chromosome abnormalities are 30 per cent more likely to become criminals than are other people. Lejeune maintained that because of this Hugon should not be held responsible for the prostitute's murder. The court disagreed. It found Hugon guilty and sentenced him to seven years in prison.

In the year that followed, the validity of Lejeune's argument was not conclusively proved or disproved, but the weight of the evidence seemed to be against any direct link between crime and the XYY pattern. The most recent investigations indicate that XYY is not as rare among noncriminals as had earlier been believed. One Canadian survey, by geneticist Fred Sergovich, suggests that the pattern may occur in one of every 250 males. If so, the idea that an extra Y chromosome inevitably causes antisocial behavior becomes untenable; there are not that many criminals. Sergovich pointed out that "if you look only at abnormal populations, you will find only abnormal XYYs."

Apart from the criminal-inheritance theories, there are two other biological approaches that have attracted wide interest. Both discount the idea that criminal behavior, or a tendency to it, is an inherited characteristic, but they do hold that a person's current biological condition may lead him to commit antisocial acts.

One of these theories associates hormones, the chemical messengers that control bodily processes, with violent criminal behavior. Psychologist Kenneth Moyer maintained that "particular hormone balances make the human system touchy or sensitive to the type of situation that might evoke attack."

The other theory links violent criminal behavior to brain damage. Psychiatrist Marvin Ziporyn, one of the main advocates of the theory, held that it explains the sensational case of Richard Speck. Early in life, the Texas-born Speck had a telling epithet tattooed on his arm: "Born to raise hell." A sometime merchant seaman, construction laborer and truckman's helper, as well as convicted burglar and forger, Speck was known as a man who was rough with women, especially when he had been drinking. In 1966, he walked into a Chicago apartment house occupied by a group of student nurses. Six were at home, and Speck herded them into a large closet and told them to lie down on the floor. Then he slashed a sheet into strips with his knife and bound the young women hand and foot. Hearing footsteps, he crouched behind a door, waylaid three more girls as they returned from dates, and tied them up. Then he freed one girl at a time, took her into another room, and began a savage orgy of stabbing and strangling. In all, he massacred eight nurses. One saved herself by rolling under a bed, where she lay forgotten.

Speck was eventually sentenced to 400 years in prison. There, he spent his time painting pictures and looking after two sparrows that prison authorities allowed him to keep in his cell. He was no trouble to anyone. "Everything is 'Yes, sir' and 'No, sir' and a smile on his face," the assistant warden told reporters.

Before Speck's trial began, psychiatrist Ziporyn spent over 100 hours interviewing him. In a book written afterward he quoted Speck at length: "When I was playing in a sandbox I hit myself on the head with a claw hammer. Accidentally. I knocked myself out. Then, a few years later—I must have been about 10—I was playing with some kids. They chased me and I climbed into a tree. I . . . lost my hold. I fell on my head. My sister found me. She thought I was dead." Speck's tale of head injuries continued: "About five years after that, I did it again. . . . I was running down a street and ran my head into a steel awning rod. I was knocked out again." In Ziporyn's opinion "Speck was a killer because his brain was damaged," and he reached the conclusion that the "lethal outburst was inevitable."

The organized search for a psychological rather than a biological explanation for criminal behavior began toward the end of the 19th Century, when the workings of the mind began to be perceived by pioneers in the fields of psychology and psychiatry. The theories resulting from this approach held that crime was often either an alternative to mental illness or a symptom of it.

The crime-as-alternative hypothesis holds that some people turn to lawless behavior in order to keep their mental balance; if they did not break the law, they would be driven by frustration to develop signs of emotional disturbance. To W. H. Allchin of Great Britain, a delinquent act is a nonverbal SOS that translates, "Somebody help me lest I go crazy." Following a similar line of thought, the American psychiatrist Seymour Halleck saw crime and mental illness as two possible responses to profound feelings of helplessness and hopelessness. The despairing sufferer may unconsciously choose crime because it makes "a more direct impact on the environment" and gives the wrongdoer a sense of being the master of his fate. "During the planning and execution of a criminal act, the offender is a free man," Halleck wrote. "He is immune from the oppressive dictates of others since he has temporarily broken out of their control."

To many other behavioral scientists, crime is not a substitute for mental illness but an expression of it. These theorists argue that criminals are often emotionally sick people whose crimes are symptoms of underlying emotional disorder.

Take shoplifting. This crime is frequently the work of professionals who make a living by stealing to their customers' specifications, or, less often, of amateurs with little money, few scruples and an intense desire to own luxuries. Such shoplifters are not necessarily emotionally ill; they steal because it pays. Others, however, take things they could easily pay for and perhaps do not even want; these offenders may suffer from kleptomania, a neurotic, irresistible impulse to steal. Karl Menninger noted that such stealing "is almost never done for the purpose of acquiring the thing taken." More often, he wrote, the kleptomaniac steals for two reasons. In a symbolic way, he is taking the love that life has denied him. He is also getting back at the world for depriving him of ordinary affection. "Taking unto ourselves and for our own use that which was once a belonging or a part of some other person is destructive in a double sense," Menninger explained. "It adds to one's self the object taken, and at the same time symbolically robs, strips, mutilates, or destroys a part of another person."

A kleptomaniac whose case lends support to Menninger's theory has been described by psychoanalysts Franz Alexander and William Healy. They wrote of Sigrid Amenson, a woman well brought up, intelligent, striking in appearance, and capable of attracting cultivated and highly educated friends even though her own formal schooling had been cut short at the age of 14. Amenson admitted that she had been stealing ever since she was seven or eight. She did not excuse herself on grounds of financial need; indeed, she said she stole more at times when she held a good job than when she did not.

"Nothing in my life that I have ever cared for have I been able to get, and that's why I feel like stealing," Amenson told Alexander. "If my mother had ever taken me in her arms and loved me, I should have been a different girl, I should have melted." In addition, Amenson apparently used theft as a substitute for sex. She thought of herself as doomed to be sexually disappointed by men, and she had so much guilt about erotic behavior that she found it more anxiety-provoking and less satisfying than stealing. Her bouts of thievery often began with tension and "a bursting desire which makes me sick." The act of stealing was always accompanied by tremendous excitement, ending in bodily trembling and, finally, in feelings of relief and physical exhaustion.

Four of the commonest urges and emotions underlying many crimes are a profound feeling of guilt, a wish for punishment, a need to assert individuality or masculinity, and an impulse to retaliate for real or fancied wrongs.

Freud called guilt "the real motor of crime." He believed that most

Criminologists suspect that the aristocrat above, Queen Victoria's grandson the Duke of Clarence, may have been Jack the Ripper, the killer who terrorized London in 1888 by slashing to death five prostitutes. A memoir revealed years later suggests that Scotland Yard knew the Duke was the murderer, but to avoid embarrassing the Crown destroyed clues and quietly sent him to a mental hospital.

people are plagued by an "obscure sense of guilt" stemming from the Oedipus complex: "the two great criminal intentions of killing the father and having sexual relations with the mother." Crime, Freud thought, provides substitute gratification of these forbidden wishes and at the same time gives the lawbreaker something to feel guilty about that he can easily understand.

Freud formulated this theory after numerous adults who were ordinarily law abiding told him about crimes they had committed as children or as adults. His psychoanalysis of these patients indicated that they had committed the crimes "precisely *because*" they were forbidden and because doing them led to a sense of mental relief. Of that kind of criminal, Freud said, "He suffered from an oppressive feeling of guilt, of which he did not know the origin, and after he had committed a misdeed, the oppression was mitigated. The sense of guilt was at least in some way accounted for. Paradoxical as it may sound, I must maintain that the sense of guilt was present prior to the transgression, that it did not arise from this, but contrariwise—the transgression from the sense of guilt."

A corollary to the idea of guilt as a spur to crime is the theory that some people become criminals because they feel an unconscious longing for punishment. Theodor Reik put it bluntly: "The prospect of punishment does not deter the criminal, but unconsciously drives him to the forbidden deed." Other experts think that it is not so much guilt as the need for attention that motivates certain criminals to court punishment. In such cases, according to psychiatrist George Solomon, the lawbreaker believes that punishment is the only form of attention he can hope to evoke from an otherwise indifferent world. Still other psychiatrists suggest that a person who would like to commit suicide but cannot bring himself to do so may murder in the expectation of being condemned to death. For instance, a frequently suicidal sculptor named Robert Irwin told a psychiatrist long before he committed three murders: "I was going to kill somebody so that I would be hung."

Without denying that guilt and a need for punishment motivate some criminals, some psychoanalysts also believe that certain antisocial acts spring from the lawbreaker's need to assert himself. Menninger cited the example of an Australian youth of 19 who tried to kill a prominent political figure and then explained to the police, "I realized that unless I did something out of the ordinary I would remain a nobody all my life." In Classical Greece, Herostratus put a torch to the famous temple of Artemis at Ephesus because, he said, he wanted to make sure that his name would be known throughout the ages.

Crime can do more than bolster a faltering sense of identity and individuality. It can also ease unconscious doubts about personal courage or sexual adequacy. Psychologist Robert Lindner found these causes prominent in his study of Harold, a young penitentiary inmate notable for a long record of burglaries and holdups.

Harold himself made the classic Freudian interpretation of the gun as a symbol of the penis, and he explained to Lindner why he sometimes brandished a weapon when he was around girls. "I-I wanted to—show them I was—better than most men, that I had great strength and—manliness. I—wanted—to show them—I had a big—a powerful penis," Harold said. "Why did I steal?" he asked himself, and supplied the answer: "I wanted to prove to myself that I could do it. I always wanted to prove to myself that I could steal something and get away with it; that I was a better man than my father thought I was. I'd think better of myself then." He added, "I wouldn't walk around with my head down when I committed a crime. I'd keep it up."

Harold believed he had once stabbed a man to death, and he confessed the deed to Lindner. Eventually, Lindner and Harold learned that the stabbing victim had not died. But his recovery did not alter the fact that the object of Harold's attack was a stand-in for his hated father. "As far back as I can remember, I didn't like my father," Harold told Lindner. "I hated my father enough so I killed the other fellow in his place. That did the job."

But, of course, the criminal's retaliatory urge may reflect something more than oedipal frustrations. It is now widely recognized that any kind of mistreatment of children may lead them to antisocial behavior as adults. A loveless upbringing, Menninger reported, helps to explain the case of the hate-filled criminal quoted at the beginning of the chapter. "At twelve he was a prisoner in a Boys' Industrial School where official cruelty added to the bitterness of his childhood years," Menninger wrote. "Subsequently, his life was simply one incident after another of revenge, recapture, punishment, release and more revenge, more punishment, more bitterness." Concluded Menninger: "The injustices perpetrated upon a child arouse in him unendurable reactions of retaliation which the child must repress and postpone but which will sooner or later come out in some form or another." It may be significant that more than half the members of the Fortune Society, an organization of ex-convicts, report being severely abused in childhood.

Psychological theories of crime causation seem persuasive to the psychologically minded, but not to everyone else. It is clear that mistreatment as a child or jealousy of a father become glib excuses cynically exploited by very practical criminals to escape punishment, so they may continue a way of life that suits them while it harms society. Beyond this perversion of useful insights are reservations about the basic validity of psychological theories of crime. Some psychologists and psychiatrists are charged with ignoring the role that social factors play in causing crime. They are also said to have based their hypotheses on inadequate evidence gathered while studying offenders who are not typical of most criminals.

It is necessary to look outside the criminal as well as inside if crime is to be explained. A growing number of criminologists believe that some of crime's causes may even lie in the victim himself. "In many crimes, especially in criminal homicide, the victim is often a major contributor to the criminal act," said sociologist Marvin Wolfgang.

Street-wise juveniles shove a shiny car toward an isolated spot in Naples where they can strip it of salable parts. Like countless children around the world, they learned criminality from their peers. Association with older toughs who steal taught the boys not only to commit such crimes but to accept them as normal.

"Except in cases in which the victim is an innocent bystander the victim may be one of the major precipitating causes of his own demise."

Wolfgang made a detailed study of 588 slayings that occurred in Philadelphia, and found that 150—more than one fourth—were what he considered "victim-precipitated homicides." By this he meant that they were killings in which the person eventually slain was "the first in the homicide drama to use physical force." Wolfgang gave a number of examples. Among them: "A drunken husband, beating his wife in their kitchen, gave her a butcher knife and dared her to use it on him. She claimed that if he should strike her once more, she would use the knife, whereupon he slapped her in the face and she fatally stabbed him." Concluded a crime commission in the United States: "What people have to fear most from crime is in themselves: their own carelessness or bravado; their attitudes toward their families and friends; toward the people they work for or who work for them; their appetites for drugs and liquor and sex; their own eccentricities; their own perversities; their own passions."

Blaming the victim for crime still links cause to an individual. But to many criminologists, and ordinary citizens too, crime is less an individual problem than a social one. The chief causes, they believe, are to be found outside the criminal, in the culture in which he lives. According to sociologist Frank Hartung, there are two views about how the culture may breed crime. The first sees the criminal as "a normal person in a normal society whose criminal behavior is learned in a process of symbolic communication with other human beings." The second hypothesis, Hartung says, holds that "the criminal is a normal human being, but he is today living in a disorganized society which tends to disorganize its individual members."

Much criminal behavior is learned through example, according to sociologist Edwin Sutherland, in just about the same way that other kinds of behavior are learned—by spending enough time at an early age in intimate contact with experts, in this case people who break the law and believe in breaking it.

But simple association with criminals is not enough to teach criminality, according to Richard Cloward and Lloyd Ohlin. An apprentice lawbreaker needs to meet the right people if he is going to get ahead. "A delinquent who is rising," wrote Cloward and Ohlin, "might begin to come in contact with mature criminals, law-enforcement officials, politicians, bail bondsmen, 'fixers' and the like. As his activities become integrated with the activities of these persons, his knowledge of the illegitimate world is deepened, new skills are acquired, and the opportunity to engage in new types of illegitimate activity enhanced. Unless he can form these relationships, the possibility of a stable, protected criminal style of life is effectively precluded."

The novice criminal finds his best opportunities for inspiration, learning and making the right contacts in what sociologists call delinquent, or criminal, subcultures. These are minicultures within larger cultures. In them, criminal values predominate, and criminal models for would-be lawbreakers to emulate are easy to find. A successful criminal, reminiscing about the role models he had found long before in his own delinquent subculture, recalled, "When I was twelve, we moved into a neighborhood with a lot of gangsters. They were all swell dressers and had big cars and carried gats. Us kids saw these swell guys and mingled with them in the cigar store on the corner. Jack was the one in the mob that I had a fancy to. He used to take my sis out and that way I saw him often. He was in the stick-up rackets before he was in the beer rackets, and he was a swell dresser and had lots of dough. . . . I liked to be near and felt stuck up over the other guys because he came to my house to see my sis."

Marvin Wolfgang maintained that some criminal minicultures deserve to be called subcultures of violence because their members see not just law breaking but assault and even murder as fairly routine matters. The use of violence in such subcultures, Wolfgang said, "is not necessarily viewed as illicit conduct, and the users therefore do not have to deal with feelings of guilt about their aggression."

Subcultures of violence exist in many parts of the world. In Colombia, for example, homicide has long been the principal cause of death among males between 15 and 45; the so-called *violencia* led to the deaths of 200,000 to 300,000 people within 15 years. Colombian guerrillas of the 1970s raided rural areas from time to time, committing sadistic murders for no clear-cut motive, and some Colombian parents taught their children specific methods of killing people.

Subcultures like that of Colombia can hardly be considered normal. Learning criminality under such conditions is a response of a normal individual to abnormal surroundings. There are many kinds of abnormalities that can have such an effect. They do more than merely permit the development of lawlessness, actually channeling people into such behavior. In a sick society, the society itself may be the main cause of crime. The 19th Century French criminologist Jean Lacassagne seems to have had something like that in mind when he said, "A society gets the criminals it deserves."

Chapter 2

Teen-age runaways sleep on benches in a New York City police station after being picked up for streetwalking. Unstable family lives drive many runaways from home and, forced to fend for themselves, they turn to criminal solicitation.

56

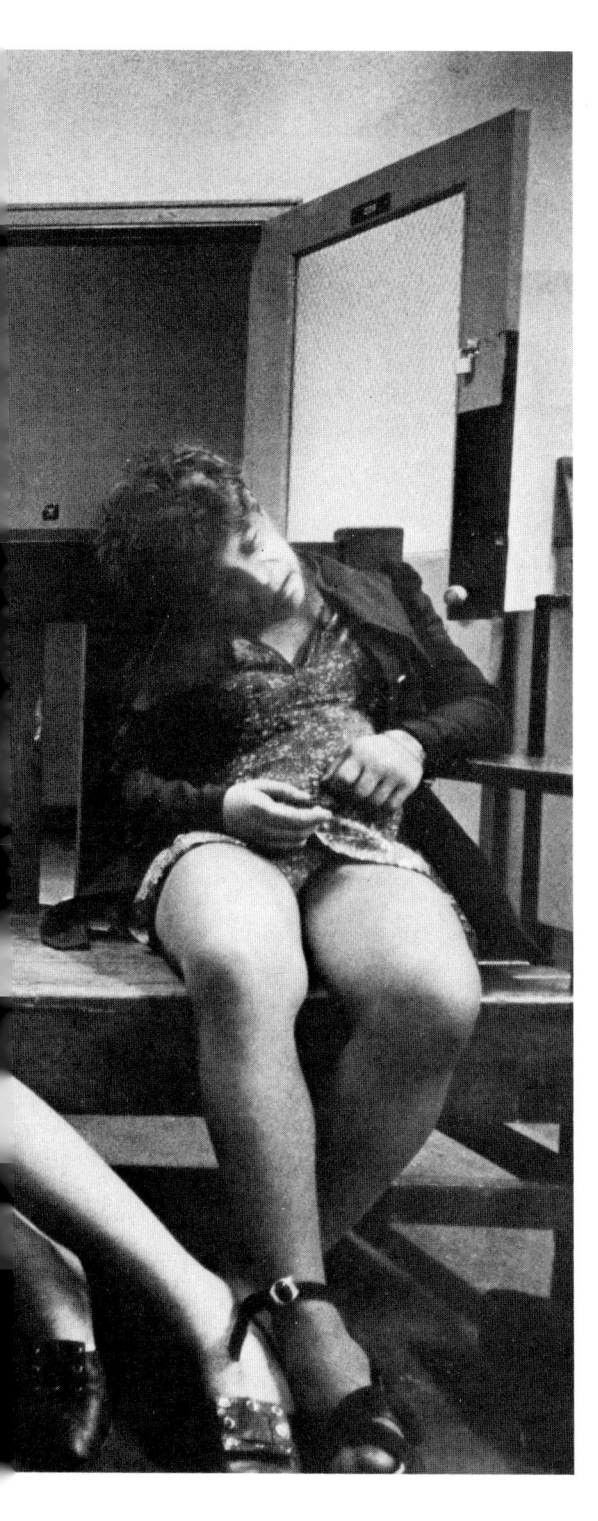

Among the social ills most often cited as causes of crime are poverty, racial discrimination and the disintegration of traditional mores. In the Fifth Century A.D. a Latin historian called poverty "the mother of crime," and its noxious effects were cited by Sir John Fortescue in the 15th Century, Sir Thomas More in the 16th and a host of behavioral scientists, social reformers, politicians and writers in the 20th. In *Manchild in the Promised Land*, Claude Brown described a young black prostitute named Dixie who "started tricking when she was thirteen." He wrote: " 'Nice' ladies used to point at her and say, 'Oh, ain't that a shame.' But it wasn't. The shame of it was that she had to do it or starve. When she got hip and went out there on the street and started turning tricks, she started eating and she stopped starving."

Virtually all studies confirm that poverty and antisocial behavior tend to occur together. Statistically, people in the lower socioeconomic classes are more likely than members of other classes to commit crimes. They are also more likely to be suspected, arrested, prosecuted, convicted and imprisoned.

But correlation is not the same as causation. "The crime rate in slums is indeed higher than elsewhere, but so is the death rate in hospitals," wrote Ernest van den Haag. "Slums, like hospitals, attract people selectively. Both are locations, not causes."

Besides, the idea that poverty is a direct cause of crime cannot account for "upperworld" crime. It cannot, for instance, explain the band of well-to-do Philadelphia youngsters who made a game out of theft. Each boy contributed some money to a pool and then agreed to steal a car. The pool went to the boy whose theft was first reported on a radio news broadcast.

A more serious flaw in the theory of poverty as a cause of crime is that it ignores a crucial fact: most poor people are not criminals. Chinese ghettos in American and European cities traditionally have low crime rates. So do Pakistani ghettos in Britain. So did the old Jewish ghettos of Europe. Even in the most crime-ridden of slum areas, law-abiding citizens make up the vast majority of residents—and are the chief victims of a criminal minority.

In short, poverty itself does not cause crime. But many sociologists believe that resentment of poverty may do so. "The problem is not not having—the immigrants did not have anything," sociologist Gilbert Geis maintained. "The problem is being told you can't be happy without having." In a sense, that idea is at the heart of Robert Merton's views, which hold that when a culture greatly values success, especially monetary success, but denies equal opportunity to everyone, the contradiction is so disorienting that some people will use illegal ways of going after what they have been made to feel they must have. Criminal anthropologist Benigno di Tullio of Italy said that his country's consumer mentality creates a sense of deprivation in some of its less privileged members that leads to crime. In France, one criminologist wrote, "The steps in the social hierarchy are so blocked up in many professions and in many classes that youth becomes exasperated because they cannot see how to climb them."

Another social ill frequently cited as a cause of crime is racial discrimination. Most studies of antisocial behavior in minority groups have dealt with American blacks, but the facts are probably similar for persecuted minorities in all countries.

In the United States the crime rate for blacks is higher than for whites. No reputable scientist has ever suggested that blacks have any innate tendency to become criminals, although prejudiced persons would like to think that they do. It is easy to refute them. For one thing, a high crime rate is not characteristic of all black groups, as it would be if criminality were an inherited black characteristic. Economically secure blacks have a far lower crime rate than poor blacks, and a similar differential occurs between well-educated and poorly educated black groups. Murder rates are several times lower in certain black African tribes than among black or white Americans. "If it needed stressing, here is overwhelming evidence that it is culture and not biological factors which makes for a high homicide rate among American Negroes," anthropologist Paul Bohannan observed. "The fundamental causes of crime in the Negro are the same as in any other group," sociologist Guy B. Johnson maintained. "The simple fact of race is not sufficient in itself to explain any important group differences in criminal behavior."

In the United States, prejudice helps keep blacks at the bottom of the social and economic heap, where most common crimes are committed. But the very recognition that discrimination and poverty are factors in crime may itself lead to a harmful social disorientation. Old standards of behavior—wrongful ones, in some cases—are set aside, and new standards do not fill the gap. The loss of traditional values may contribute to crime. Urbanologist Edward Banfield decries the 20th Century moral climate in which disadvantaged groups are widely thought to have "a kind of quasi-right to have their offenses against the law extenuated, or even to have them regarded as political acts reflecting a morality 'higher' than obedience to the law." Making much the same point, psychiatrist Frederick Hacker says: "It's reached the point where there are no criminals in San Quentin anymore. They're all freedom fighters."

More serious is a general questioning of what is right and what is wrong. Albert Bandura, a former president of the American Psychological Association, is certain that many people are more tolerant of crime, especially violent crime, than they once were. He mentions the tendency to belittle the objects of violence (to call policemen "pigs," for instance) and to sanitize terms for violence (for example, to speak of "wasting" instead of "killing").

The disruption that follows the loss of traditional values is obvious, but neither it nor poverty and discrimination can explain most antisocial behavior. In fact, sociological theories that look only outside the criminal for the causes of crime are just as vulnerable to criticism as biological and psychological theories that look only for internal causes. The point was summed up by Halleck. "Just as psychiatry has failed to account for the selective criminality of individuals with similar personality traits, so has sociology been unable to account for the selective criminality of individuals exposed to similar social situations." Not everyone who owns a gun uses it; not everyone who associates with criminals, or lives in poverty, or comes from a broken home ends up as a criminal.

The truth, Stanton Wheeler suggested, is that virtually all theories of criminal causation "suffer heavily from a lack of adequate supporting data." They have not been proved, and it is probably impossible to prove them. Crime seems too complex to be explained by any one theory. But if causes cannot be pinned down and better understood, much about crime can be, with potentially useful results. Many criminologists now bend their major efforts toward learning how criminals operate and how those operations might be prevented.

60

Insights from the arts

To the creative mind, the drama of crime has proved irresistibly fascinating. In novels and poems, plays and films, the genius of centuries has been poured into portrayals of the criminal impulse, the criminal mind. The roster of artists whose perceptiveness has provided revealing insights into criminal behavior includes towering classic playwrights Sophocles and Shakespeare *(whose Othello appears at left)* as well as the 20th Century French novelist Albert Camus and film makers Fritz Lang and Charles Chaplin.

Their works are not detective stories, whodunits in which the trick is to guess who committed the crime. The criminal is the hero, and the question to be resolved is why. The great artists have tried to penetrate the reasons behind aberrant behavior, to trace the often labyrinthine motives that forced the hero to his actions.

In their analyses, writers and film makers have foreshadowed the conclusions of modern criminologists, who reject simple explanations for crime. The causes are many, experts say, often mixed and mysterious in origin. It is exactly in portraying the deep and tangled flaws in a man's personality, the profound sources of evil in his society, the wellsprings of destructiveness lodged in human nature itself, or perhaps all of these working together that the artists have excelled. They have delved into the human soul and have revealed—as contemporary criminologists would also maintain—that an impulse toward crime lurks in the dark recesses of every psyche.

Shakespeare's Othello, played by Paul Robeson, declaims his remorse over the body of his wife, Desdemona, whom he has just murdered in jealous rage, while Lodovico waits to arrest him for the crime. Othello, a fine man and brave soldier, kills Desdemona because he is too rash. His suspicions aroused by the villainous Iago, he does not stop to think but suffocates his innocent wife.

The hero with a tragic flaw

Macbeth (played by Michael Redgrave) shows Lady Macbeth (Flora Robson) the bloody daggers he used in killing Duncan, King of Scotland.

Greek playwrights and Shakespeare all lived in heroic times, and their tragedies reflect this, portraying heroes who, although great men, commit heinous crimes through fatal flaws in their characters. Shakespeare's Macbeth is a man of courage and ambition—too much of both, for they lead him to murder. Sophocles' Oedipus *(right)* also falls from an excess of bold decisiveness. Although warned by an oracle that he will kill his father and marry his mother, he rashly murders an elderly man and marries an older woman, fulfilling the prophecy. He blinds himself in remorse.

Douglas Campbell, masked like an ancient Greek actor, plays Oedipus, who committed the heinous crimes of incest and patricide.

Portraying society as the villain

Dickens' Oliver Twist watches a juvenile thief, the Artful Dodger, pick a pocket.

The imagination of English novelist Charles Dickens was haunted by crime, and crimes haunt his books. But Dickens had the 19th Century faith that the human heart was good and that crime arose from social evils—poverty, deprivation and slums where even small boys learned to be criminals. In *Oliver Twist*, the homeless Oliver is taken in by a gang of pickpockets and is schooled in their trade by a deft delinquent called the Artful Dodger.

In movies, Charles Chaplin has also blamed crime on the injustice and brutality of society. In the alum-bitter comedy *Monsieur Verdoux* he plays a man who marries a series of rich women and kills them for their money. If business is a form of murder, he implies, why not make murder a business?

Chaplin, playing the bluebeard Verdoux, woos actress Margaret Hoffman, one of the succession of wives he makes it his business to kill.

Evil born in a twisted mind

The psychopath M, portrayed by Peter Lorre, uses a glimpse of toys to entice a young girl whom his mental illness impels him to kill.

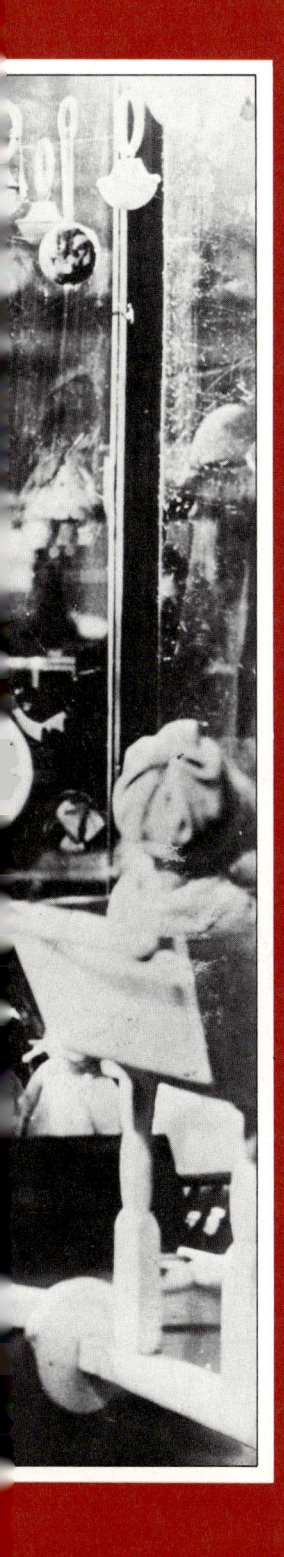

In a woodcut by Fritz Eichenberg, Dostoevsky's Raskolnikov dreams of the axe murder his twisted mind drove him to commit.

The 19th Century Russian novelist Feodor Dostoevsky created in *Crime and Punishment* the deepest, most penetrating study of the tangled psychological motives that stand behind many crimes that, critics agree, can be found in all literature. The mind of Dostoevsky's murderer-hero Raskolnikov is a maelstrom of painfully conflicting emotions. He is tormented by poverty, by feelings of shame and inferiority and powerlessness. He must strike back at the world that, he feels, humiliates him daily.

In conflict with these feelings is the hysterical conviction that he is a superior being, a superman who has the right to kill inferior beings. So he lashes out, splitting the skull of a loathesome old moneylender. Then Dostoevsky shows how Raskolnikov's tormented conscience forces him to make incredible blunders that inevitably draw the attention of the police and make him a prime suspect in the killing. His conscience finally forces him to confess.

Fritz Lang in his film *M* also treats the psychologically tormented criminal with great understanding and sympathy. His main character is a psychopath who commits dreadful crimes: he kidnaps and then murders little girls. Yet Lang shows that the criminal himself suffers horribly from his affliction and is filled with remorse for his crimes.

Coleridge's Ancient Mariner, dead albatross hung round his neck, tries to pray on his cursed ship among dead crewmates.

The mystery of motiveless violence

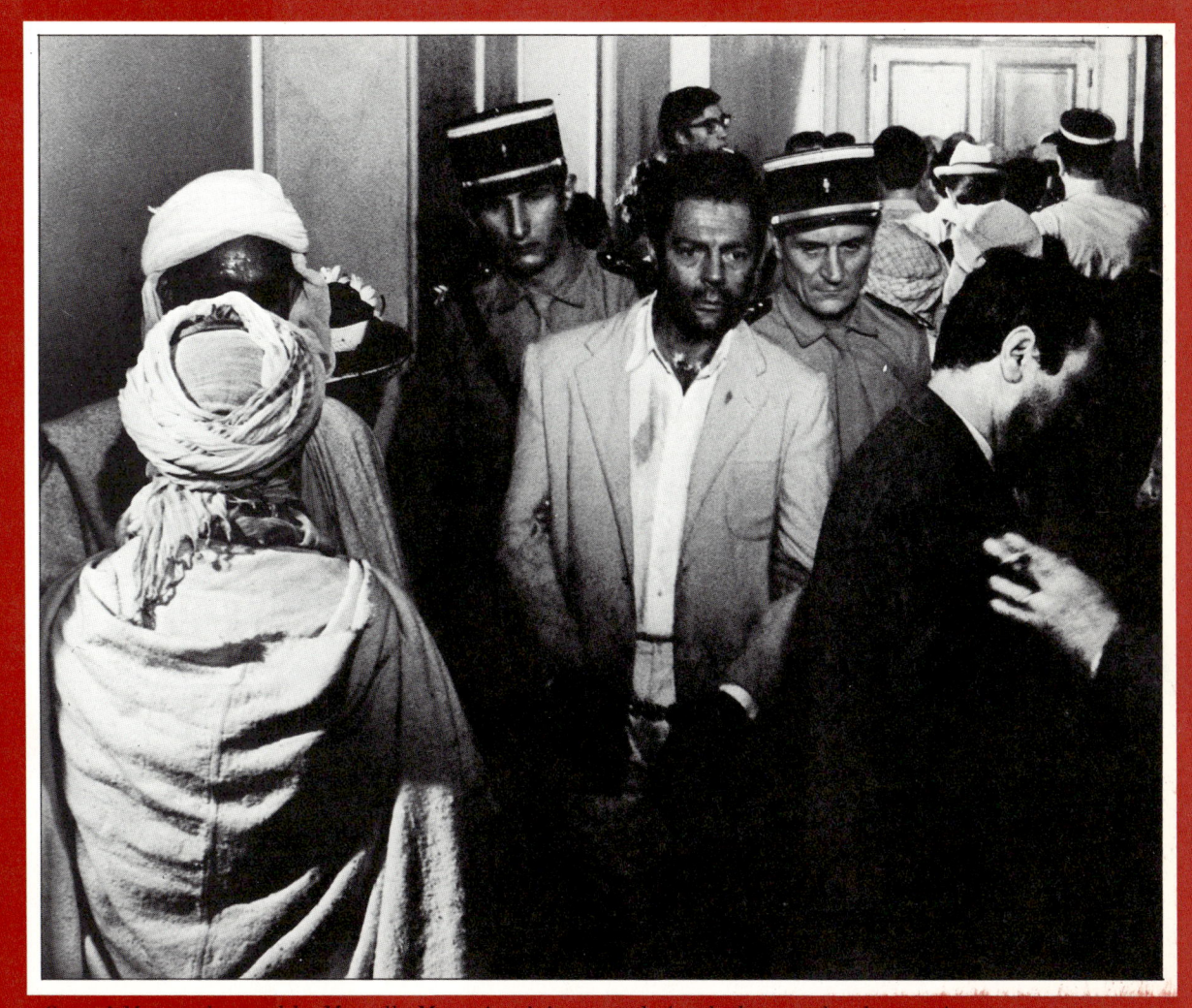

Camus' Meursault, acted by Marcello Mastroianni, is arrested after he has murdered a man for no apparent reason.

To many people today, life itself lacks meaning, and consequently crime needs no explanation: it just happens. As far back as 1798, the poet Coleridge foreshadowed this view of crime in *The Rime of the Ancient Mariner*. His mariner wantonly shoots a beautiful bird, an albatross, thus, Coleridge says, sinning against God. But the mariner's worst sin is the spiritual emptiness that brought him to commit the crime.

It is only in the present century that this feeling of alienation has become a principal element in the artist's analysis of crime. In Camus' *The Stranger*, the chief character, Meursault, kills a man for no apparent reason. But, Camus goes on to show, Meursault's entire being has been stifled and twisted by a feeling of alienation. His crime, like the Ancient Mariner's, is a cry of protest against the emptiness of life.

69

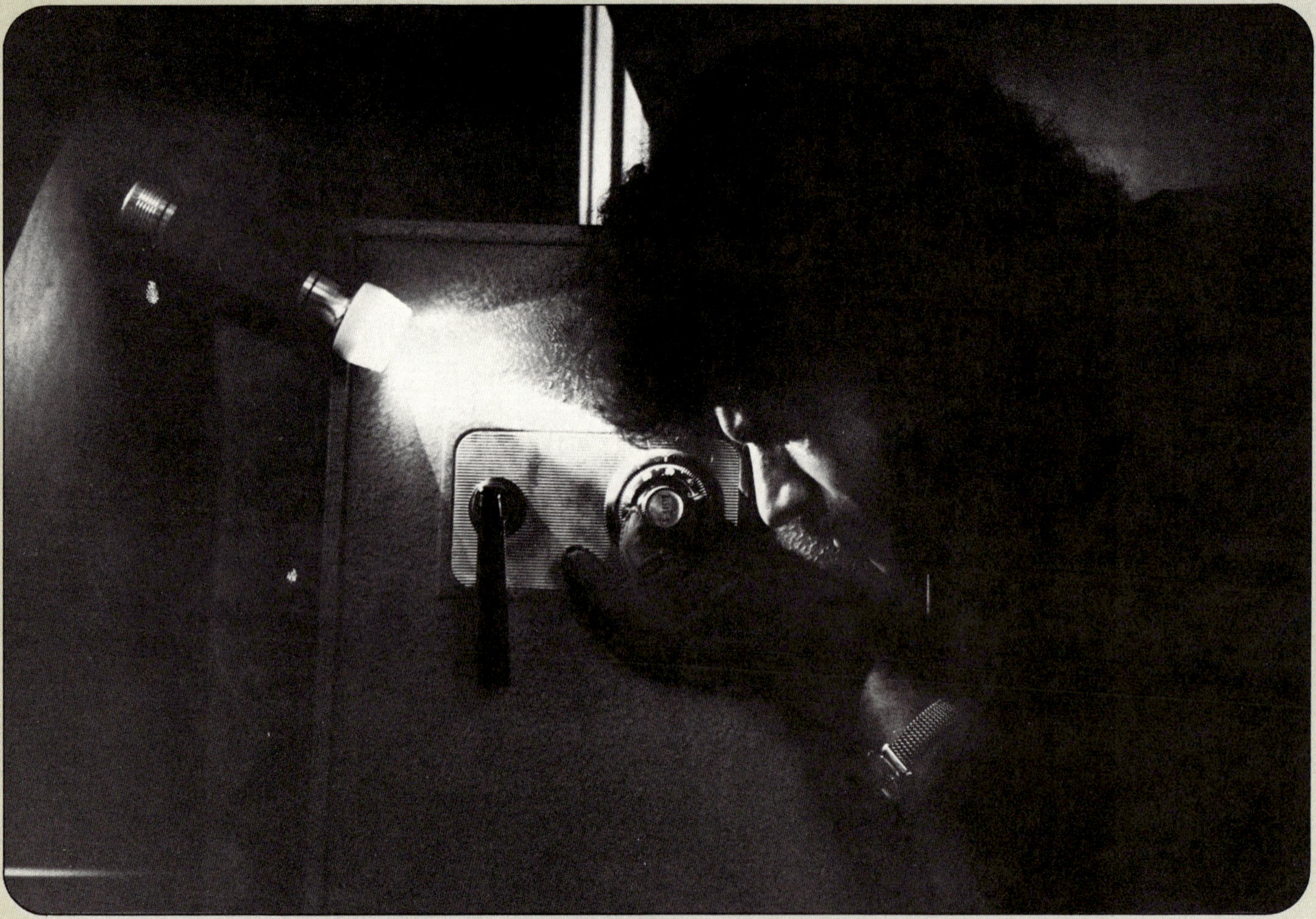

The Professionals

3

Many of the characteristics of the professional can be seen in Herbert Emerson Wilson, whose criminal career is illuminating if not exactly typical. Wilson, an American, was an ordained clergyman for 20 years, but he was never happy in this respected, low-paying profession. In midlife he took the bold step of changing careers. He decided to become a safe-cracker, confident that his new field would bring handsome financial returns. Before his criminal career ended, he dynamited his way into 65 safes and vaults from which he extracted $15 million.

Wilson's new career was launched when he bought a copy of *How to Be a Detective,* a book on common errors made by criminals, which he used as a how-not-to guide to crime. Then he had the good fortune to meet a specialist in burglar alarms and vaults, one Herbert Cox, with whom he formed a solid partnership. Wilson developed his own safe-cracking skills methodically. He got a temporary job in a factory that manufactured safes; he pretended to be in the market for a safe so that he could pump retail dealers about the burglar-proof features of various makes, and he practiced in his garage until he could open a vault —as he later put it—with "no more noise than a pig's grunt."

By now Wilson was ready to storm such seemingly impregnable objectives as a Kroger supermarket safe that not only stood in a brightly lit window but was under the eye of an armed guard who waved an hourly greeting to a policeman on his beat. Wilson later described the assault step by step. "We made a dummy safe which was an exact duplicate of the Kroger box. The phony cardboard safe was a beauty, complete with wheels, combination door, hinges and gold lettering, and was constructed so that it could be taken apart."

Wilson and his aides got into the store at night through a coal chute to the basement. "The night watchman never knew a thing until we shoved a rod in his back. He had on a pretty blue uniform with a neat little gun belt—the fanciest guard I ever saw—and he squawked plenty when we made him strip. I couldn't blame him, because I know how silly a man feels standing around in his underwear, but we needed that suit. Herb Cox put it on and went right into the watchman's routine. We had one man patrolling the street and another at the rear door with a buzzer on which to give us signals."

Sawing a hole in a partition behind the real safe, they lassoed it, pulled it back out of sight, and substituted their own creation. Wilson went to work. Suddenly, "Three buzzes, the danger signal, hit me like a scream out of the night. Nobody moved. Nobody breathed. But there was a noise. Somebody tapping. I knew what it was, and my stomach was jumping. 'Herb!' I called to Cox. 'It's the damm' beat cop. Get out there!' 'Get out there? You mean plug him?' 'Hell-no! Show yourself. Stay out of the light but let him see the uniform. Wave at him.' Cox stumbled out like a sick man, hugging the shadows for support. I felt for him. I was scared cold myself. But he did it. He waved at the cop, and the cop, glancing at the dummy safe, waved back."

Wilson's account was openly boastful. "Looking back over my record, the Kroger job seems a masterpiece and I'm proud of the ingenious way we beat that mark. But actually it was a risky venture. We rarely made a foolish move and we had a system that kept us out of jail for years," he said. "We got our fifteen million because I insisted on discipline and careful planning."

This tale highlights traits that sociologists have discerned in certain criminals: conscientious professionalism, pride in competent performance and ability to plan and execute undertakings that demand intelligence, self-discipline and restraint. The vast majority of crimes are committed by ordinary people, amateurs who steal or kill once and never again—not necessarily because of any remorse over violating the law but because circumstances do not impel a repetition. Yet some of the most troublesome crimes are committed by professionals, people who consistently break the law. For them crime is a livelihood, often a highly specialized one. David Maurer, of the University of Louisville, has interviewed scores of such lawbreakers, and his description of this type gives a good idea of the full-time lawbreaker's personality and his world: "The professional works at crime as a business; he makes his living by it; he is recognized and accepted by other professionals in his class as a professional; he knows and uses the argot or semisecret language of the profession; he subscribes to the code of behavior long established for professionals in his group; he has status and is known within a considerable circle of other professionals." Finally, concluded Maurer, "He feels no shame or guilt for his acts against the dominant culture, and seldom if ever 'reforms.'"

While the elite among professional criminals are expert technicians, most lawbreakers are not. If they specialize too much, they miss too many opportunities to turn a dishonest profit. When sociologist Leroy Gould and his colleagues asked professional criminals just what they did, the investigators were told over and over again, "I hustle." To hustle, Gould explained, "is to be persistently on the lookout for an opportunity to make an illegal buck. A criminal 'on the hustle' . . . will consider whatever comes up." The President's Crime Commission found that in the United States "hustling means moving around the bars and being seen; it means asking 'what's up.' It means 'connecting' in the morning with two others who have a burglary set up for the evening, calling a man you know to see if he wants to buy 10 stolen alpaca sweaters at $5 each, and scouting the streets for an easy victim. It means being versatile: passing checks, rolling a drunk, driving for a stickup, boosting a car, burglarizing a store."

Hustlers gather at particular bars and restaurants that function as job-placement centers. "These centers," the Crime Commission explained, "do for the professional criminal what want ads, employment offices, and businessmen's luncheons do for legitimate business. Through contact with other criminals, professionals learn of jobs to be pulled and of openings in groups planning to pull them. Contacts of this type also enable the professional to keep abreast of the latest techniques."

Although new technology—the invention of new tools or weapons, for instance, or the development of the computer—gives criminals new ways of operating, it does not create brand-new criminal professions. Maurer finds that "every principle of thievery known today was chronicled by Petronius as he surveyed the Roman underworld; the principle of every confidence game operated in our own times is . . . recorded in the great mass of picaresque literature which flooded Europe during the 16th and 17th Centuries; these principles were already ancient and timeless, it should be noted, by the time they were written down."

Many sociologists divide professional criminals into two main categories: the "heavies," who employ violence and the threat of violence, and the "grifters," who depend on wit instead. The heaviest of the heavies are the hired killers. Pike Ryan was one such, practicing his profession as a member of the Whyos gang in New York City in the mid-19th Century. When he was finally arrested, he was carrying a price list in his pocket that offered a whole range of services. "Punching" cost $2, "nose and jaw broke" $10, "ear chawed off" $15, and "doing the job" $100 and up.

Chapter 3

The commonest type of heavy criminal in many countries, however, is not the killer but the armed robber, for whom murder or mayhem is secondary to the primary aim of theft. And among the most troublesome in the Americas, where the violence rate is high, is the urban mugger. Jones, the mugger whose portrait James Willwerth painted in a book of the same name, is one example.

Jones grew up in a ghetto, the son of a white nurse and a black postal worker struggling to rise to the middle class. He aspired to a career as a singer, but by 17 he was a thief. He had fantasies of making one huge haul that would give him a start in the legitimate world. "I'd have a country home," he said, "but I would never go there, of course, because I don't like the country." He was thoughtful and—atypically—ambivalent about his lawlessness. "When I hit—steal from—a dude, I feel bad for him. But I am doing a job. . . . I know it's wrong. But this gets me what I need. Life is based on survival, and self comes first. . . . I don't feel that I'm a crook. I have a job the same as you."

Jones's defensiveness did not interfere with his expertise. "The best time to mug a person is in the daytime. That's because the people around don't want to get involved," he explained. "In the daytime, people are always rushing somewhere."

He paid attention to his appearance. "If you look like a bum, you stand out." Jones never looked like a bum. "People think you are waiting for a date. So they sleep on you. You look like you've got a job. My gold ring is a good thing to play on; it looks like I have money, so nobody thinks I am a mugger."

Jones always tried to be sure in advance that he would get something for his trouble. "You lay outside a bank, or a check-cashing place; you know the dudes have cash. . . . Today, like, I watched faces going in and out of this bank. Tomorrow I'll go back again. If I see those faces again, I'll know they aren't going to the bank for themselves. So I'll pick a face and follow it to its store. As a rule, stores make one drop a day. They usually make these drops between two and three o'clock. I'll time this dude for a few days. Say he's pretty close to between two and two-thirty. I make it my business to be there."

Jones never attacked precipitously. Mugging, he believed, was like chess, which was one of his favorite games. "You try to stay a few moves ahead of the dude you are going to hit; you can't let him know you are setting him up. You are deep into planning the way it will happen, and the big thought is that he might not go along with your scheme. You don't want a big scrap because that brings cops. You want to get in and get out fast."

Practiced with such attention to detail, Jones's profession netted him between $10,000 and $20,000 a year, tax free. But it frequently made him anxious. "Fear is the thing. I don't know what *he* knows, and he don't know what I know. It's like going into a fight. I don't like it because I don't like to fight. At heart, I don't want to hurt nobody—I don't want to be hurt myself."

If Jones's carefully reasoned techniques demonstrate the proficiency of a lone criminal, Britain's Great Train Robbery of 1963 is an unusual example of the expertise involved in large-scale heavy crime. The robbery required a year of planning. It brought together 15 men, all experienced criminals, though some of them had legitimate sidelines; one ran an antique shop, for instance. Each was assigned a specific role in the robbery, and technical tasks, such as uncoupling one railroad car from another, were well rehearsed. The group even bought a farmhouse

A ski-masked gangster presses a gun into the back of a hostage, threatening to kill him unless a demand for $2 million in ransom is met by Paris' Credit Lyonnais bank. The job was pulled off with professional skill—until the very end. The bank provided the money, but as the robber fled, his car collided with another; in the ensuing tussle, police killed him.

near the tracks to use as a base before and after the holdup.

On the night of August 8, 1963, the assault was launched. Scouts patrolled with walkie-talkies to guard against surprise. One man put a trackside telephone out of commission so the intended victims would be unable to summon help. To stop the train, another specialist masked a green signal and activated a red one with batteries. When the train came to a halt, the thieves separated the engine and the cash-loaded car just behind it from the other cars. Then they drove on up the track to a lonely spot where automobiles and a truck for the getaway had been parked. The gang's expert locksmith had little trouble getting into the railroad car. Inside, it was no trick at all to overpower the mail clerks and relieve them of the 124 mailbags in their care. These proved to contain about what the gang's preliminary research had led them to expect: two and one half tons of banknotes adding up to more than two and one half million pounds (some seven million dollars).

There was one flaw in an otherwise perfect performance. A single member of the gang failed in the responsibilities that had been assigned him: removing all traces of the robbers' presence in the farmhouse once they had left. By some incredible oversight, there were fingerprints everywhere, and they proved the undoing of the robbers, most of whom were caught and sent to prison.

The train robbers' willingness to use violence—they bludgeoned the locomotive engineer and threatened other crewmen—marked them as heavy criminals and distinguished them from the nonviolent type of lawbreaker, the grifter. Wary of physical force, grifters depend for their success on special technical skills.

Three important kinds of grifter are the booster, or professional shoplifter, the pickpocket and the confidence man. In terms of status, the booster is at the bottom of the heap; other criminals look down on him. A big-time confidence man said of a shoplifter he knew, "While he is undoubtedly a professional thief, I should have been ashamed to be seen on the street with him. . . . My reputation would have suffered in the eyes of my friends to be seen in the company of a booster."

Yet the booster is master of a demanding set of skills. Unlike the snitch, or amateur shoplifter, the booster steals to sell and has to perfect his technique to earn a living. To remove labels that could incriminate him if he is caught, he may practice manipulating manicure scissors inconspicuously, or learn to use a razor blade that can easily be discarded if necessary. Or he may design a "booster box" for stolen articles. An empty box wrapped for mailing and slit along one edge makes a good hiding place for phonograph records. A briefcase

Hooded, handcuffed and heavily guarded, three participants in the Great Train Robbery in England in 1963 leave court —betrayed by the kind of stupid slip that even professionals make. The robbers got seven million dollars in a deftly executed coup. But they left fingerprints in a hideout and were readily identified.

with a hinged side is useful for shirts and sweaters, while a larger container with a spring closing can hold a typewriter. What store detectives call "bad bags," shopping bags imprinted with the store's name, are valuable to the shoplifter. So are "booster skirts or pants," ordinary-appearing garments with baglike compartments inside.

One successful female booster relied less on equipment than on personal talents. She was an excellent actress who pretended to be a bad-tempered shopper in search of bargains. "Sales clerks who knew her type vanished on seeing her," wrote criminologist Mary Owen Cameron. And she was so adept at changing her appearance that store detectives who thought they recognized her were never sure enough to challenge her. She was caught only when a suspicious detective called her by name. The booster turned around—and was arrested.

Most professional shoplifters work in troupes of two or three. The "stall" is the person who "throws a hump," or distracts the attention of clerks by asking to be waited on, pretending to faint, starting a small fire or engaging in some other maneuver. The "clout" does the actual stealing, and the "cover," if there is one, conceals the clout's exit or carries the stolen goods out himself.

This kind of operation is very old. Cameron quoted an English description of shoplifting written in 1597 in which only the language seems outdated: "The higher degrees and gentlemen-lifts have to the performance of their faculty three parties of necessity, the lift, the marker and the santar. The lift, attired in the form of a civil country gentleman, comes with the marker into some mercer's shop . . . and there he calls to see a bolt of satin, velvet, or any such commodity, and, not likeing the pile, colour, or brack . . . he calls to the mercer's man and says, 'Sirrah, reach me that piece of velvet' . . . and whilst the fellow turns his back he commits his garbage [stolen goods] to the marker. . . . The marker gives a wink to the santar, that walks before the window. . . . 'Sir, a word with you. . . .' 'Truly sir,' says the santar, 'I have urgent business in hand, and as at this time I cannot stay.' 'But one word, and no more,' says the marker, and then he delivers to him whatsoever the lift has conveyed to him; and then the santar goes on his way, who never came within the shop, and is a man unknown to them all."

As ancient a grifter's trade as shoplifting is pickpocketing. Success depends on exceptional skill. The best, noted David Maurer, have "raised the business of stealing from a victim's person to a high art in which timing, bodily contact, the psychology of misdirection, *grift sense*, the use of concealment both personal and extrapersonal, the rhythm of movement, speed and an impressively delicate dexterity are all blended into a single, almost instantaneous, and practically invisible act." Although some pickpockets manage alone, most have one accomplice; in Europe they often operate in troupes. In a two-man operation one person is the "tool" (American argot) or "claw" (the British term), who "hooks," or does the stealing. The other is the stall, who maneuvers the mark. "The stall, working from signals given by the tool," explained Maurer, "holds the victim in position with his body, using his upper arms, his back, his elbows, or his legs to block any movement the mark may make, and to keep the mark's hands clear of the pocket to be picked; this is called *framing the mark*, or *putting up for the mark*."

Not all pickpockets find stalling congenial. One expert put it this way: "I learned to stall and I learned to hook too, and I broke in many a stall. A lot of stalls won't break in, you see, because they're thieves and they won't be told. That's the reason they are thieves. They don't want people to tell them what to do. So if you can't tell a man what to do, then he can't stall."

Stalling is considered the more demanding of the two pickpocketing subspecialties, but the tool's work is also difficult. "Hooking his index finger just within the *crack* of the pocket, he takes up a pleat in the lining, then makes a dozen or so tiny pleats, folding the lining with great dexterity between his fingers. This is called *reefing* or *reefing a kick*," wrote Maurer. "His hand does not go into the pocket at any time, but the shortening pocket-lining moves the roll of bills upward so that it emerges at the mouth of the pocket."

Like any profession, pickpocketing has its negative side. In the eyes of some criminals, it is not a particularly high-status occupation. Swindling is. The confidence man, whatever his fraud, enjoys the esteem of professionals in other fields. According to sociologist Edwin Schur, "The con man is generally recognized to be at or near the top of the underworld's status hierarchy. In part this is due to the sheer skill his job involves, and his ability to score without recourse to the use of weapons and threat of violence employed by professional 'heavies.' " Alexander Klein explains further: "Every deception, every imposture is an assumption of power. The person deceived is reduced in stature, symbolically nullified, while the imposter is temporarily powerful, even greater than if he were the real thing."

The swindler's task is basically the same in all confidence games. He must stir his victim's greed and then convince him of a sure-fire scheme for getting a lot of money in return for a relatively small outlay.

Some con men think big. Joseph Weil *(page 46)*—an American swindler known as Yellow Kid after a cartoon strip character—took eight million dollars during a career spanning more than four decades by selling bankers worthless oil stocks. Weil went to elaborate lengths to establish impressive, if fake, credentials. Sometimes he rented a lavish office that exuded respectability and success. Sometimes he submitted forged letters of recommendation from well-known businessmen. Sometimes he impersonated an established financier, displaying copies of a magazine article with his own photograph substituted for a real celebrity's. Weil suffered not a twinge of conscience over his victims' losses. "They wanted something for nothing," he said; "I gave them nothing for something."

But most swindlers are small-time operators. There still are carnival workers who bilk patrons at fairs and traveling shows of small sums with rigged gambling games. Some employ a gaff, a hidden mechanism that keeps customers from winning games billed as tests of skill. The "stick" is an accomplice who plays the role of a satisfied customer and entices marks into playing gaffed games. And the alibi agent is an expert at a rigged game called alibi. Its name comes from the agent's habit of giving the mark an explanation for every failed attempt at winning. For instance, the agent may comment, "You threw that one too high," implying that the mark can win if he buys another chance.

There are two ubiquitous criminal specialists who are neither heavies nor grifters although they are definitely professionals. These are the pimp and the prostitute. The oldest profession may alter its form to suit the time and the culture, yet it has flourished persistently in every complex society simply because it provides a service that is generally illegal but powerfully desired. What motivates its practitioners—many of them highly intelligent—has been debated for millennia by priests, philosophers, politicians and scientists.

One view of modern prostitutes is the simple one held by Harry Benjamin and R. E. L. Masters: a few choose prostitution because of strong sexual appetites, but most are driven to "the life" by emotional instability or choose it because they find it an easy, seemingly glamorous way to earn a living—not merely a fate better than starvation, but an opportunity to rise above poverty or a pinchpenny middle-class struggle. Benjamin and Masters described one call girl—a university-educated former teacher—who took to prostitution because of her "powerful desire for 'the good things.'" She told them "she would 'rather die' than go back to her old life." This girl may not have been entirely typical. The investigators concluded that, just as "one encounters rather few prostitutes who are neurosis-motivated," so there are, in the United States, few white prostitutes "who are entirely free of neurotic elements, and who have chosen their careers on an altogether rational basis."

The motives that lead a woman to become a prostitute are only as complex as those binding her to her pimp. The link between the two is more than a simple business partnership. Some psychoanalysts think that the prostitute is held to her pimp because she is lonely. Others believe that what keeps the pair together is unthreatening sex; many prostitutes are frigid, many pimps at least latently homosexual. Still other analysts are convinced that what the prostitute wants from her pimp, and believes she has in him, is someone even lower than she. As French analyst Maryse Choisy put it, they "do not unite to love, but to hate."

Some confirmation for that view can be found in the studies of pimps made by anthropologists Christina and Richard Milner. In long con-

continued on page 84

Bonnie Parker, America's most notorious female desperado, flaunts her pistol as she leans on a getaway car she and Clyde Barrow used for holdups. Bonnie and Clyde terrorized the Southwest for two years, robbing banks, groceries, service stations and jewelry stores, and committing at least a dozen murders before being killed in a police ambush in 1934. Their biggest haul was $1,500.

A gallery of legendary rogues

To some of the professionals who make crime their lifework, spectacular success brings a kind of notoriety that enshrines them in popular legend. A few achieve such grudging admiration because of their skill and ingenuity. Others, even though they may be sadistically cruel killers, catch the public fancy with their foolhardy courage.

Although the cigar-chomping Bonnie Parker *(above)* and her partner Clyde Barrow were cold-blooded murderers, many of their robberies were directed at banks—victims few persons feel sorry for—with dash and élan.

More subtle was Willie Sutton, a master of the art of disguise, who conned his way into many bank vaults.

Elmyr de Hory fleeced the wealthy even more artfully—by successfully selling his superb forgeries of masters of modern art. Yet for all their skill and daring, these professionals—like most other criminals—finally got caught.

Celebrated art forger Elmyr de Hory fastidiously finishes a painting in his studio. He specialized in works by modern masters, and palmed off a thousand fakes as the productions of Picasso, Matisse and others. His craftsmanship was such that he once got $115,000 for a fake Derain from a New York gallery.

Willie Sutton, a highly successful bank robber, is booked in New York City in 1952. Sutton, a consummate professional known as "The Actor" for his use of disguises, is supposed to have explained he robbed banks "because that's where the money is"—although he later denied that he had made the statement.

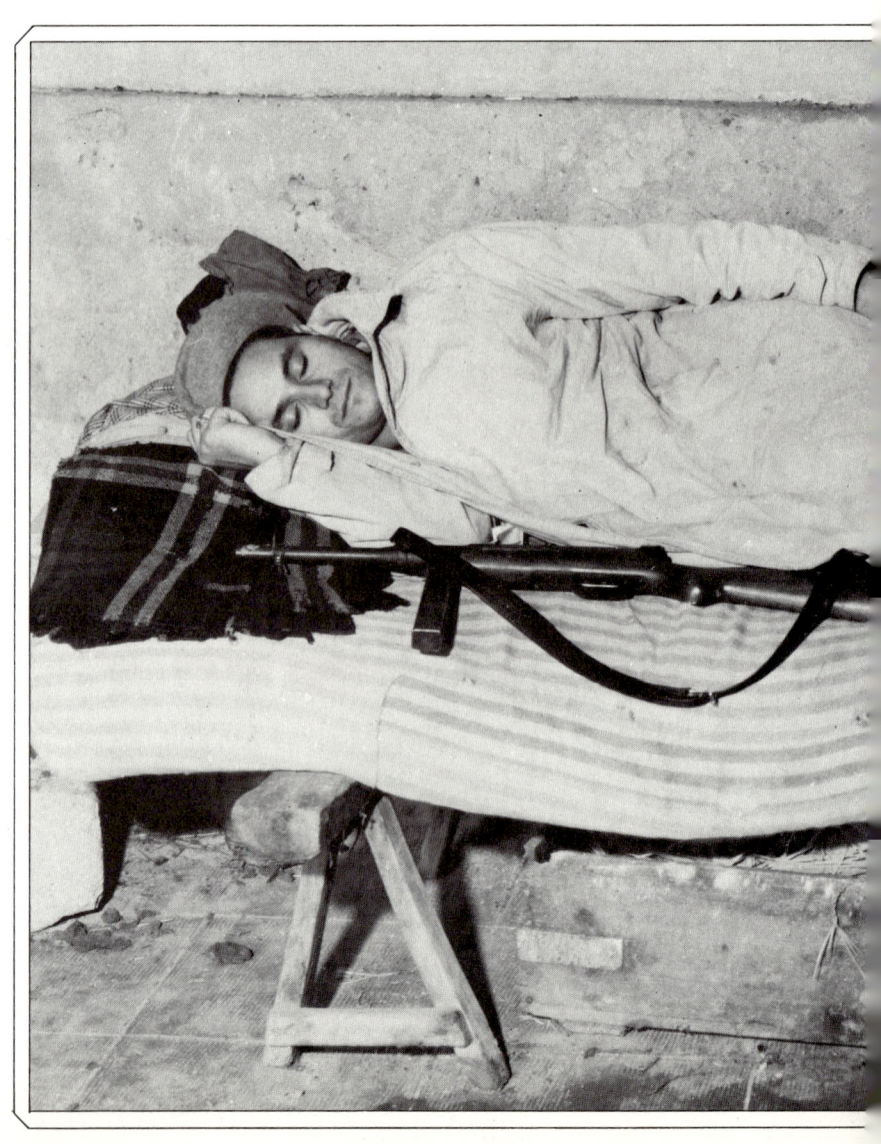

Sicilian bandit Salvatore Giuliano sleeps peacefully—but with a gun nearby—in his hideout in the hills. Many Sicilians revere him as a modern Robin Hood who shared his loot with the poor. This is doubtful. What is certain is that he committed some 300 crimes during the 1940s and was not caught until betrayed by an accomplice. He was shot in bed.

After success as lightweight boxers, the Kray twins, Reg (left) and Ron, became heavyweight criminals, muscling into various London rackets. Their most lucrative was extortion—backed up by beatings and killings—to force nightclub owners to pay for protection. Their criminal careers ended in 1969 when they received life sentences for murder.

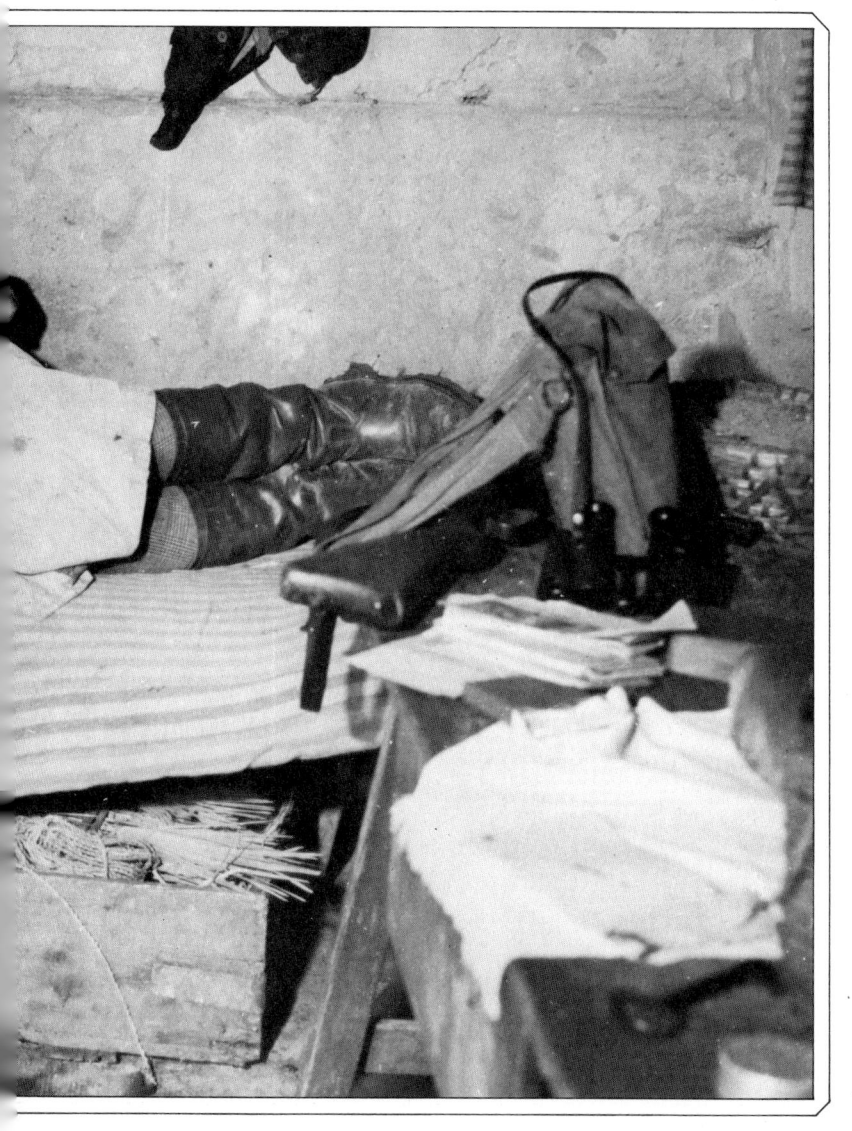

versations, a former pimp known as Iceberg Slim proposed to Mrs. Milner that successful pimping requires hatred of women. "That's where the thrill was," he said, "in the absolute vilification, in the degradation. I had this intense hatred. To be a great pimp, I think you've really got to hate your mother."

The pimps, or "players," interviewed by the Milners found their careers deeply satisfying. They enjoyed the deference that they exacted from their "hos." One required every ho in his stable to light his cigarettes and speak only when spoken to. Gesturing toward his favorite, he said, "Notice how quiet she is. You know why she's quiet? 'Cause I'm talking, not because she has nothing to say. She's as smart as I am, or smarter; she got two degrees. But she's a quiet, humble, beautiful woman because she knows the position of her place, she likes it."

But to the pimps as well as the prostitutes, the life was basically a business, its chief attraction, the money and luxuries it provided. A pimp became positively eloquent about the jewels one of his fellow professionals wore to a party. "There was one cat out of Miami, believe it or not had a diamond between his teeth, that's right. Had his ears pierced, had a diamond hanging out of his ear. Now that's what I call a lover of the stone or a connoisseur of nature."

Neither pimps nor prostitutes are gangsters, but in many cases their ties to organized crime have been close. Prostitution is highly profitable, and it has been at various times an attractive investment for criminal syndicates. The syndicates can arrange for services essential to prostitutes and pimps—hotels and brothel buildings, legal assistance and, most of all, some protection from police harassment. It was the business of operating chains of brothels that helped establish the criminal organizations of many notorious American gangsters of the 1920s and '30s, including Al Capone and Charles "Lucky" Luciano.

Such big businessmen of crime make up the upper class of professional lawbreakers. They are set apart from others not simply by their wealth and power but by their method of operation. Working relationships between professionals are generally transient. Two or more criminals may come together to do a particular job, but they usually separate when it is done. "The chances of their forming a stable mob are slight," wrote Leroy Gould. By contrast, organized criminals are members of large and enduring organizations. Each organization has a recognized hierarchy of authority, is structured and run like a legitimate business firm, and may be tied to other illegal groups in a kind of criminal cartel. While such syndicates are most active in the United

States, their counterparts exist in almost every country. The origins of the *boryokudan*, or violence organizations of Japan *(Chapter 1)*, can be traced to the 16th Century, when some unemployed samurai formed small gangs and began committing acts of banditry. Like members of the Mafia, they took a blood oath of fidelity to the *yakuza* (outlaw) code, and even today, a *yakuza* atones for a breach of his oath by cutting off his little finger and offering it to his *oyabun* (boss).

For 300 years, Japanese gangsters tried to maintain a Robin Hood image. They gave to the poor, scrupulously avoided harming the innocent, and in public took obsequious pains to avoid stepping on anyone's shadow, as polite etiquette required. In recent years, however, they have turned to thuggery and displays of power. It is reported that when an *oyabun* named Ichiro Ishii got out of prison, 300 subordinates donned elegant black suits and gold stickpins and gathered en masse at the Tokyo railroad station. As Ishii stepped down from the train, they bowed deeply and cried out, "Welcome home!" Then they proceeded to Ishii's headquarters in a 30-car motorcade, while other gangsters directed traffic with walkie-talkies. And when Genichiro Sakata, another *oyabun*, was due for release from prison, 110 of his followers chartered a jetliner so they could greet him at the jailhouse door.

In Hong Kong the Triads, separate criminal gangs derived from ancient, respectable secret societies, control drug traffic, extortion, gambling and prostitution. An estimated 80,000 of the colony's four million residents belong to Triad groups.

In Continental Europe the most important criminal organization is the Union Corse, a secret underworld society that originated in Corsica but is now headquartered in Marseilles. During the early 1970s, the Union Corse was widely believed to dominate world drug traffic. In France it exerted powerful political influence, partly because some of its members worked in the Resistance during World War II and in 1948 helped the French government break a strike in the port of Marseilles.

During the 1960s, two crime families operated in Britain. The Richardson mob was headed by two quiet brothers, Charles and Eddie, while the flamboyant Kray twins, Ronald and Reginald, along with their brother Charles, led a second gang. Both groups had two specialties, long-term fraud and extortion. Long-term fraud, explained Sir Richard Jackson, one-time assistant commissioner of Scotland Yard, "entails starting a business, ordering goods from the wholesalers, and paying for them almost at once. Then, once confidence has been established, the swindler starts giving larger orders and obtaining longer credit. Finally he sells the goods for cash and absconds with the proceeds." As

Chapter 3

Women smugglers, their knapsacks stuffed with cigarettes, trudge through an Alpine pass leading from Switzerland into Italy. Such smuggling of highly taxed goods has for centuries been a profitable—and respectable—livelihood for men and women who live near the mountainous frontier areas of Europe.

extortionists, the Richardsons and the Krays demanded protection payments from nightclub owners or insisted on taking a cut of some businessmen's profits.

In addition to such tightly organized gangs in Europe, reported criminologist John Mack of Glasgow, there is "a loose network of mutual acquaintanceships and friendships" that functions more effectively in illegal trade than the European Economic Community in legitimate commerce. Stolen jewelry and furs are sold and resold along a trade trail that begins in Germany and leads through Belgium, the Netherlands and Spain to Italy. There illegitimate factories use the stolen goods as raw material for new articles that can be sold through legal channels.

Commerce in stolen cars is particularly well planned and brings together the efforts of professionals in several countries: planners, thieves, technicians and mechanics who can alter a vehicle's appearance, forgers, document counterfeiters and drivers to transport the cars over one or another trade trail. One of these routes has its start in Germany and winds through Austria and Yugoslavia into Turkey and Lebanon. Another runs between Sweden and the Netherlands, while a third goes from Sweden to Germany.

In 1969, police broke up a 74-man operation that had flourished for two years under the joint auspices of three different gangs. German and Italian thieves first stole expensive cars—Mercedes and Porsches were favorite targets—in the posh ski resort of Kitzbühel, Austria, or in Munich, Paris or Rome. Several garage owners, accomplices of the thieves, saw to it that the cars were disguised, while two teams of forgers drew up new identifying documents. Then each automobile was driven across the border of the country where it had been stolen and sold through newspaper advertisements to wholesale dealers or private buyers.

Syndicated crime in America wields power on a much vaster scale than anywhere else in the world. In the United States, according to the President's Crime Commission, "Organized crime is a society that seeks to operate outside the control of the American people and their governments. It involves thousands of criminals, working within structures as complex as those of any large corporation, subject to laws more rigidly enforced than those of legitimate governments. Its actions are not impulsive but rather the result of intricate conspiracies, carried on over many years and aimed at gaining control over whole fields of activity in order to amass huge profits." Those profits have been estimated at $40 billion a year, higher than the net income of any one legitimate industry and twice the amount "earned" by lawbreakers who operate outside organized crime.

Some experts think there is no such thing as a nationwide association of criminals. Many criminologists and most law enforcement officials think otherwise. "There is overwhelming evidence that an organization variously called 'the Mafia,' 'La Cosa Nostra' and 'the syndicate' operates in the United States," sociologist Donald Cressey wrote. However, its efficiency and pervasiveness, other experts believe, are overrated.

Although criminal gangs long had been influential in American cities, they did not become big business until 1919, when Prohibition created both a tremendous thirst for illegal liquor and the opportunity for a new "service trade," in the words of Gus Tyler, syndicated columnist and crime observer. "A business as big, complex, risky, and capital-hungry as the bootlegging of alcohol in the 1920s demanded cartelization," Tyler pointed out. "Hijacking had to be eliminated on both land and sea. The coast guard, customs, and the police had to be bought *collectively* to avoid double payment and double cross. The market had to be allocated to avoid cutthroat competition and flooding. The gangs had to gang together for their mutual good: the hoods needed a brotherhood—their counterpart of the Steel Institute or the American Medical Association."

A woman shows off 10 kilos of hashish that she tried to sneak out of Turkey in 1970. Like most professional smugglers, who avoid violence, she depended on guile to trick customs inspectors—she tied the bulky drug sacks under her blouse, pretending to be pregnant. An observant official was not fooled.

Chapter 3

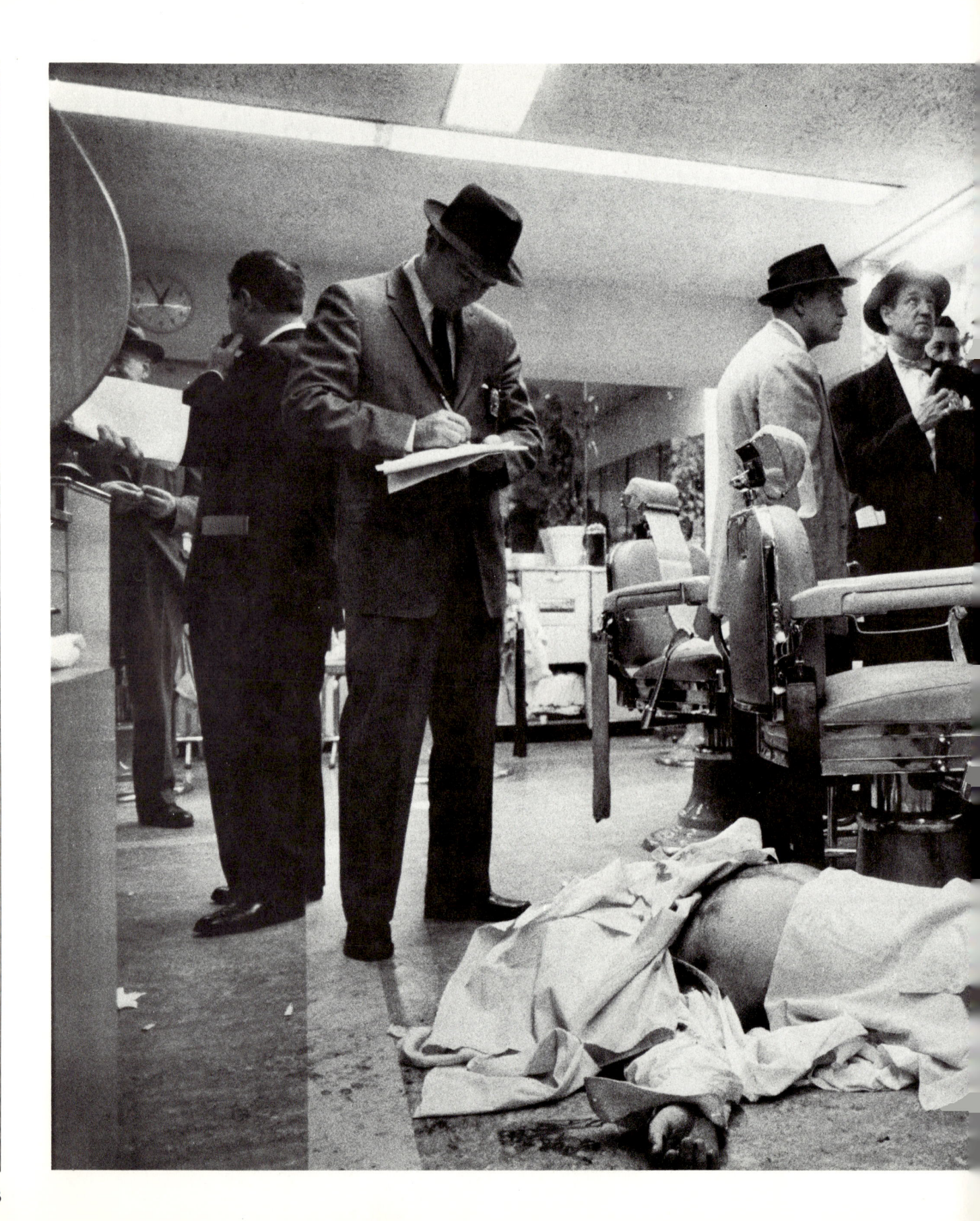

88

The shrouded body of mafioso Albert Anastasia lies on a barbershop floor in Manhattan's Park Sheraton Hotel minutes after two masked murderers fired five shots into the unsuspecting gangster while he was being shaved. Like most gangland executions, the murder was never solved, but police believe it was ordered by rival racketeers who feared Anastasia, a mobster credited with arranging more than 60 murders.

This unification was achieved after bloody fighting in the '20s, culminating in the Castellamarese war of 1930 and 1931. To put an end to the bloodshed, the leaders finally agreed to divide up the nation into separate criminal territories.

This structure has endured. At its top is a ruling commission made up of leaders who control crime in large areas—New York, New Jersey, Illinois, Florida, Louisiana, Nevada, Michigan and Rhode Island. At its heart are 24 groups linked to one another by their deference to the commission. On the periphery are numerous secondary syndicates tied to the Mafia itself by agreements.

The 24 main units have from 20 to 800 members each and are called families. Core members are related by blood or marriage, but nonrelatives belong, too. Most are descendants of immigrants from Sicily and southern Italy, but all strains of the American melting pot are represented. Organization follows the model of the ancient Sicilian Mafia. Each family is headed by a *capo* or boss, who is assisted by a *sottocapo* and advised by a *consigliere*, described by Cressey as "an elder member who has partially retired after a career in which he did not quite succeed in becoming a boss."

Below the level of the *sottocapo* come several *caporegime,* or lieutenants, each of whom, like a works manager in a legitimate firm, runs some branch of the family's criminal activities. *Soldati,* or soldiers, rank at the bottom of the family hierarchy. "A soldier," Cressey wrote, "might operate an illicit enterprise for his boss on a sharecropping basis, or he might 'own' the enterprise and pay homage to the boss for 'protection,' the right to operate. All soldiers in good standing are guaranteed a livelihood and need not fear encroachment on their illicit operations by other soldiers." Beneath them, and outside the family, are employees and agents who do most of the actual criminal work.

For two years, from 1967 to 1969, anthropologist Francis Ianni made an unusual study of a New York crime family that he came to know through his long-standing friendship with one member. Ianni gathered some information from his interviews with most of the family's 15 core members. His principal research method, however, was that of participant observation, the same approach Margaret Mead used when she investigated little-known tribes in the South Seas. As a guest at weddings, christenings and intimate family gatherings at home and in clubs and restaurants, Ianni shared in the day-to-day life of the Lupollos, as he called them. He neither took part in nor witnessed criminal activities.

"The Lupollo family is a business empire made up of a number of legal and illegal enterprises which mesh into a structure of business corporations, investments, tactics and personnel like any other corporate enterprise," Ianni wrote. The empire was held together not by criminal interests but by the bonds of kinship. Members of the family (used now in the ordinary, narrow sense of the word) shared an extreme distrust of outsiders, an unusual feeling of closeness to one another and, Ianni said, a lack of the ability "to see any morality or social order larger than their own."

These feelings were the heritage the family patriarch, Giuseppe, passed on to his two sons: Joe, who became head of the family after Giuseppe's death in 1950, and Charley, who functioned as *consigliere* to Joe. Charley explained to Ianni that "Pop used to talk to Joe and me on how important it was for the business to be protected and to make sure that we had friends who we could trust. If he told us once, he told us a thousand times that you couldn't trust the judges and the politicians to

Smartly suited Sicilian mobster Giuseppe Genco Russo (center) struts at the head of a religious procession in his hometown of Mussomeli, glorying in a position of honor his gangland notoriety helped earn him. His criminal activities enhanced his power in the noncriminal world, but eventually they led to his exile.

do anything for you. . . . Pop always said that he trusted Italians more than Americans, Sicilians more than Italians, his *paisani* more than other Sicilians but most of all he trusted his family. And family to Pop means not just those of us within the family but everybody who was related to us. Even there, however, he made it clear that blood was more important than marriage and the closer you were related to somebody the more important to have their trust."

Relationships among the Lupollos were not completely free and easy but followed strict rules that depended on each member's place in the family hierarchy. Each Lupollo was owed a certain degree of *rispetto*, or respect, and it was *rispetto* that determined protocol. "At a family social gathering," Ianni wrote, "positions at the table, order of the service and even who serves and who is waited upon, are signs of the respect afforded each man. In business matters, the right to initiate ideas and make suggestions is a function of how much respect an individual commands."

As head of the family after his father's death, Joe expected, and got, the most *rispetto*. Whenever several Lupollos decided to go out to dinner, it was Joe who chose the restaurant (and picked up the check). One refrain that Ianni heard over and over again was, "Check with Joe."

Like the Lupollos, most crime families engage in more than one kind of wrongdoing. They may be involved in large-scale theft and extortion, but their principal business is providing illegal goods and services: narcotics, gambling and loan-sharking. In recent years, syndicate criminals have also controlled a growing share of the pornography business, but their role in prostitution has diminished. Law enforcement officials say that 15 Mafia members control at least 80 per cent of the multimillion dollar drug trade in the United States—they are importers and distributors, leaving the riskier retail end of the business to small-time criminals. Even more profitable than narcotics is illegal gambling: off-track betting on horse races and various games in most states, as well as the lucrative numbers game, in which a player gambles on the last three digits of a published tabulation, such as the U.S. Treasury's cash balance on a particular day.

The Lupollo numbers enterprise is a good illustration of the businesslike methods that are employed by organized crime. Joe Lupollo, the family boss, underwrote the undertaking. Vito Salemi, who was a relative by marriage, directed, working out of a storefront headquarters variously called the bank, the main office or the regional office. Phil Alcamo, another in-law, functioned as layoff banker, transferring some bets to other operators when a particular number attracted heavy play.

There were eight semiautonomous "wheels," or district banks. One was owned, managed and financed by Salemi himself, five were headed by other family members, and two were run by outsiders who had bought franchise rights from the Lupollos. The family guaranteed the financial solvency of each wheel, providing emergency funds whenever there happened to be too many winners at once. In return, the district wheels paid a fixed percentage of their gross income to the regional bank.

At the next lower level, there were eight district controllers who, as employees of the district managers, ran the actual gambling operations. Below them were collectors, who picked up bettors' money and the slips that record every bet from local runners. The bets themselves were taken from customers by runners.

Loan-sharking, one of organized crime's major sources of revenue, means lending money at illegally high interest rates, ranging from 1 per cent to 150 per cent a week. A client of the Lupollo family's loan-sharking business explained to Ianni how it worked: "Most of the sharks are given a large bankroll. They move around the community looking for people who are in one kind of jam or another and who need money in a hurry. . . . You have loan sharks who follow all of the floating crap games that are also operated by the family. The people who play in these games play for large sums of money and when somebody is busted, a loan shark is right there to loan him money."

Small-time gamblers, too, borrow from organized criminals at times. "Factory workers who lose money to the resident bookmaker discover that the resident bookmaker is also a resident loan shark," Cressey reports. Other clients are addicts in need of money for heroin, and small businessmen who may have trouble getting an ordinary bank loan. Cressey also describes loan sharks who, "occupying higher Cosa Nostra echelons," specialize in lending to other loan sharks and to affluent businessmen. Known as money-movers, these lenders play an important role in the syndicate because they steer profits from narcotics and gambling into highly lucrative channels.

The loan-shark business has an enforcement as well as a lending side. A borrower who gets behind in his payments is certain to be threatened; he may be brutally beaten, or even killed as an example to others. Gus Tyler quoted a store owner on his encounter with the mobster who was trying to collect: "He showed me a story about a man whose body was found in Jamaica Bay with weights on it, and he said it could happen to me. He said, 'If this house gets on fire one night how are you going to get the kids out? Your whole family will go up. I know the school

Chapter 3

Exiled mobsters pose for a portrait at the penal colony on L'Asinara island, northwest of Sardinia. All except the third man

from the right, convicted of murdering Sicily's highest magistrate, are members of the Calabrian Mafia charged with a rash of kidnappings.

your kids go to; they can get hit by a car. Accidents do happen!'"

A borrower who can't repay the loan may have to turn over his entire business, or perhaps run it for the Mafia's benefit. In fact, sophisticated loan sharks like the Lupollos have increasingly used their lending operations in recent years to move into legitimate business. In addition, Gus Tyler says, "loan sharking is a way of hooking otherwise honest people to do the work of organized crime." A longshoreman who cannot pay up may be forced to help the Mafia smuggle drugs, or he may have to tip off his creditors to the location of valuable cargo that they could hijack. A businessman might have to help dispose of stolen property, while a municipal official might pay his debt by helping the syndicate get city contracts and kickbacks.

Large-scale theft, like the business of providing illegal goods and services, nets billions of dollars every year. Automobile theft is one of the major moneymakers. Pilferage, the theft of whole carloads and truckloads of goods from piers, railroads, shipping rooms and warehouses, is another lucrative Mafia activity. It is tied in with the work of big-time fences, whose merchandising operations are not very different from those of legitimate wholesalers.

Another kind of theft, the stealing and counterfeiting of credit cards, is a growing Mafia interest. Mobster Charles Teresa once described one attraction of the stolen card. With it, "a man could go into a big terminal or to a number of travel agencies and pick up $3,000 to $4,000 worth of plane tickets in an afternoon. Then he could sell them at half-price to anybody who wanted them. Some guys I know would fly from one terminal to another, all over the country, just buying airline tickets with stolen credit cards and selling them as fast as they got them."

Extortion, generally meaning the protection rackets, is another major type of syndicate crime. In the simplest kind of scheme, a businessman pays organized crime a percentage of his income as insurance against "accidents" to his person or premises. At one time, every bar owner in one Midwestern city regularly handed over 10 per cent of his gross income to Mafia henchmen. In another case, syndicate criminals demanded a 25 per cent cut from a vending-machine executive. Under more complicated schemes, the underworld does not extract direct tribute but uses force or the threat of force to make a businessman buy unneeded, inferior or overpriced supplies from a syndicate-controlled company. After muscling its way into certain labor unions or vital trades, the Mafia may force concessions from businessmen by threatening to foment labor trouble or by holding up delivery of vitally needed restaurant or building supplies.

The world of organized crime seems remote, but in the United States, at least, it affects the lives of millions of ordinary citizens. This is because the underworld uses its huge income to buy power in business, in politics and in the criminal justice system—welcomed often by respectable citizens anxious to take advantage of the gangs' extralegal resources. Crime families have invested heavily in food processing, construction, trucking, importing, restaurants, race tracks and other legitimate enterprises.

In 1952, political scientist Alexander Heard estimated that organized crime contributed about 15 per cent of all the money spent in American political campaigns. In addition, organized crime had invaded the criminal justice system at every level by bribing and intimidating policemen, prosecutors, witnesses, jurors and judges.

A taped conversation between a Chicago racketeer and a vice-control detective named Donald Shaw shows how the underworld goes about the task of corruption. Jacob Bergbreiter, a police lieutenant with ties to the Mafia, arranged for the meeting. As it happened, Shaw arrived wearing a hidden radio transmitter linked to a police car. He was asked to provide advance warning of any police raids against nightclub gambling operations. "If you . . . see something I should know, I'll give you a (telephone) number," said the racketeer. "I can decorate the mahogany a bit. . . . See what I mean? I could help with the payments on the new car. I can see that you are taken care of every month. I can see that every month there is a little worldly goods for you." Not long after the meeting took place, Bergbreiter turned up at Shaw's house and left $500 in cash. Bergbreiter was suspended from the force, but attempts to convict the racketeer proved unsuccessful.

Such efforts at bribery are successful in an unfortunately large number of instances. But corruption explains only part of the gangs' power. They have the resources to retain good lawyers, who manipulate democratic legal processes to delay or forestall conviction for obvious wrongdoing. Important members of the syndicates have records of many arrests but few—and brief—prison terms. Even if sentenced, some manage to continue to operate their illegal businesses from behind bars. As a result, organized crime is the most difficult of all professional crime to control with a justice system established to serve a free people.

Chicago's bootlegging tycoon

Organized crime exists to make money, like a legal business. And the successful illicit professional follows the same principles that guide his law-abiding contemporaries. First, he must identify an opportunity—a product or service for which there is a strong demand. Then he must make sure that ample sources of supply are available to him. Next he must devise a marketing strategy. Finally, he needs ways of dealing with the competition that will enable him to survive and prosper even while others are dropping off all around him.

When the legal manufacture and sale of alcoholic beverages was prohibited in the United States in January 1920, the opportunity was obvious. Here was a product—booze—for which there was an insatiable demand. Sources of supply, at home and abroad, could be arranged. Retail outlets, new and old, were looking for stock. The sawed-off shotgun and Thompson submachine gun provided effective means of dealing with the competition.

The super-tycoon of Prohibition-era bootlegging was Al Capone, called—never in his presence—Scarface because of a fight-inflicted wound. He was a burly, cigar-chomping mobster whose smiling countenance *(right)* masked a savage brutality. Capone established himself in the underworld as a brothel keeper, then expanded into bootlegging, and through bullying, extortion and murder became the most powerful racketeer the world had known.

When he was described as a criminal, Capone not unnaturally demurred. "I call myself a businessman," he said. "I make my money by supplying a popular demand."

A beaming Al Capone is surrounded by competitors who made the mistake of crossing his path. O'Banion, a florist by day and rumrunner racketeer by night, was gunned down in his flower shop; Genna, who controlled Chicago's illegal liquor makers, fled to Sicily; Saltis, an O'Banion henchman, retreated to rural Wisconsin; O'Donnell, one of a tough hijacking gang, was wounded by a Capone henchman and quit the rackets.

EDWARD "SPIKE" O'DONNELL

JOE SALTIS

AL CAPONE

DION O'BANION

JIM GENNA

A booming industry in illicit alcohol

With the coming of Prohibition, most brewers, distillers and liquor importers closed up. But, noted John Kobler in his book *Capone*, the respectable Chicago brewer Joseph Stenson went into partnership with Capone's gangs and kept operating. Legitimate suppliers in Canada, Scotland and France shipped whiskey and wines to U.S. shores, to be picked up by rumrunners *(right)* like Capone's enemies, the O'Banions.

Most liquor was concocted amateurishly in small stills. Police estimates put stills at over 100 a block in parts of Chicago, mostly tenement-kitchen alky cookers controlled by a Capone ally. In 1927 liquor production was said to be 12 million gallons higher than in 1917, the peak pre-Prohibition year.

Pursued by the Coast Guard, a rumrunner hastily jettisons his cargo offshore.

Under the watchful eyes of checkers, bags of illegal whiskey are unloaded from a boxcar on which they were disguised as lumber.

Workmen dismantle a 100-gallon still discovered by police in a raid on a garage. Much illegal alcohol was manufactured in unsanitary stills; the product frequently contained poisons, rats, garbage, cats, mice or cockroaches.

Retail outlets for a popular product

Like the producers of alcoholic beverages, most restaurants, bars, clubs and stores that had sold liquor before Prohibition continued to do so afterward. All were at the mercy of racketeers like Capone, who controlled the police who could raid them, as well as their essential sources of supply.

In the big cities speak-easies proliferated—there were an estimated 32,000 in New York, including the city's poshest nightclubs. Raids were frequent in some areas, but had little effect on illegal drinking. Fiorello LaGuardia—later New York's mayor—said it would take 250,000 policemen to enforce Prohibition in New York, and another 200,000 to police the police.

Without bothering to remove their hats, businessmen enjoy an eye-opener at the Brass Rail in the heart of Manhattan's business district. Drinking started here at 8:30 in the morning; whiskey sold for 50 cents a drink, and gin for 35 cents.

A schoolboy purchases a bottle of booze from a storekeeper. Many small grocery stores, tobacco shops and newsstands were fronts for a brisk trade in booze for consumption at home or in private clubs—speak-easies were relatively few outside the sophisticated cities.

Well-heeled consumers enjoy a drink at the Hunt Club, one of New York's many stylish speak-easies. The club had 23,000 members, served 700 a day and boasted that it sold the best whiskey in New York.

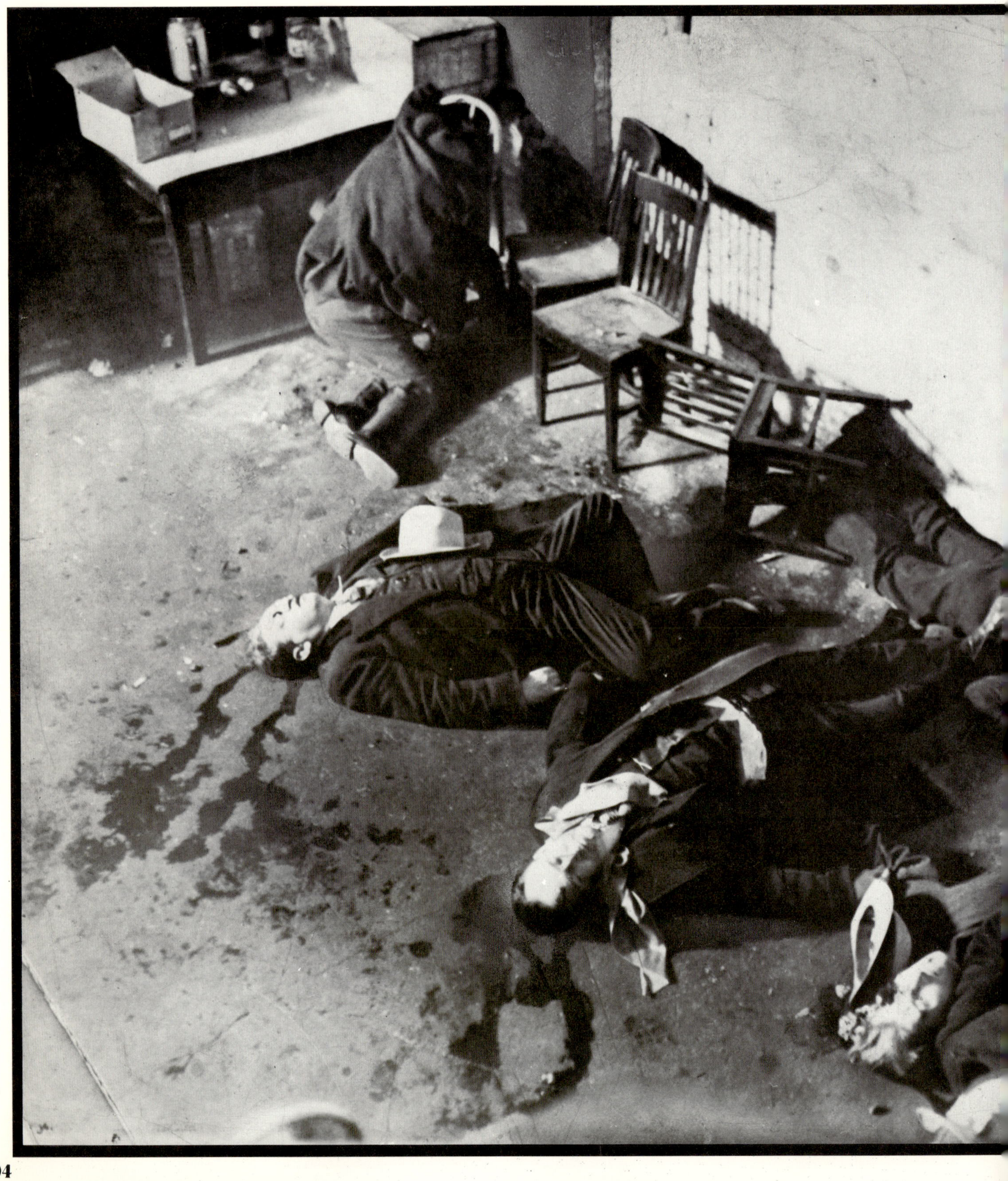

How to deal with the competition

Like any businessmen, bootleggers had to compete on the basis of price and quality. At the Capone headquarters in Chicago, samples were available for retail dealers to try.

More aggressive methods came into play if competitors lured away customers or hijacked shipments. "I don't hurt nobody," said Al Capone, "only them that get in my way." The remnants of the O'Banion mob continued to get in his way until St. Valentine's Day 1929. Then they were lured to a Chicago warehouse by the report that a truckload of hijacked liquor would be delivered there. Shortly afterward three men in police uniforms and three in civilian clothes went inside, lined up the unsuspecting gang members—they thought it was a police raid—and disarmed them. Then they raked the hapless mobsters with submachine-gun fire and administered the coups de grâce with a sawed-off shotgun.

The victims included six racketeers and an optometrist named Reinhardt Schwimmer, who was not a criminal but enjoyed the excitement of being with mobsters. "He fell into bad company," his mother later said. Capone was conveniently in Florida at the time. But he was presumed to be behind the murders: Bugs Moran, an O'Banionite who missed being in the warehouse by minutes, said, "Only Capone kills like that."

Six victims of the St. Valentine's Day massacre lie in pools of blood in a Chicago warehouse. A seventh victim survived the fusillade and managed to crawl to the door even though hit with 14 bullets. Taken to a hospital, he told a detective, "Nobody shot me," adding before he expired, "I ain't no copper."

Massive floral wreaths overflow the house, onto the front balcony, porch and front lawn after the death of Al Capone's brother Frank. Every inch of space inside the house had already been filled. As the floral tributes kept arriving, trees and lamppost were festooned with them.

A proper send-off for big-time hoods

The gangs' business operations depended on personal allegiances, often expressed in formal ceremonies. Even an enemy became a brother after he was dead, and funerals were lavish rituals. When the racketeer Bloody Angelo Genna was carried to his rest *(below)* after being gunned down by fellow hoodlums, it was as if a great potentate had died. And when Al Capone's brother Frank was killed in a gun battle with police he was buried in a satin-lined coffin and there were so many flowers that the house would not hold them.

Formally attired pallbearers carry the coffin of a murdered mobster, Angelo Genna, past a stylishly dressed throng to burial in an unconsecrated grave. Genna was one of six gangster brothers, three of whom were killed in gun battles. The other three retired to obscurity.

107

Capone's wall-enclosed winter estate was a 14-room mansion on an island in Florida's Biscayne Bay. He enjoyed entertaining show-business luminaries and civic leaders, who hailed him as "the new businessman in the community."

From rackets to riches and celebrity

Crime made Al Capone rich and famous. He bought a 14-room mansion in Florida, hobnobbed with celebrities, and was the subject of books and films. He carried $50,000 around in his pockets, and reportedly had a $15 million fund for palm greasing.

In Chicago Capone occupied a whole floor of the Lexington Hotel, kept a teen-age mistress on the floor above, and had his food prepared by a private chef (whose job included tasting it before serving). The opulently furnished executive office, Room 430, was generally filled with padlocked canvas bags of currency. Capone's multiple enterprises grossed hundreds of millions of dollars a year.

During a relaxed moment, Capone fishes in Florida waters from his cabin cruiser.

Chicago Cubs star catcher Gabby Hartnett autographs a ball for Capone's son Albert, called Sonny, as guards watch grimly.

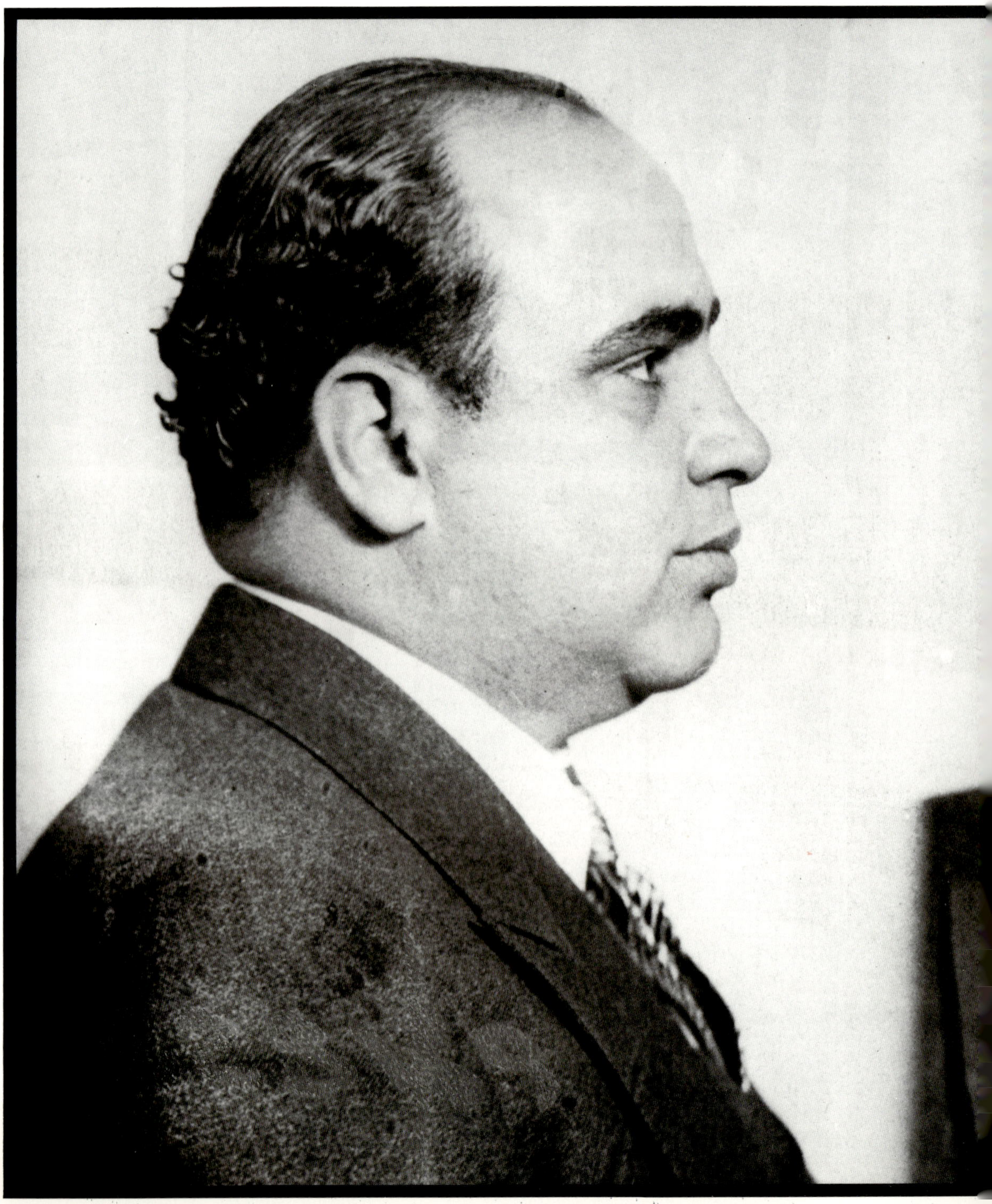

The end of an infamous career

Business success was Capone's undoing. He had been arrested many times and imprisoned once. But it took painstaking detective work, prodded by direct orders from the President of the United States, to end Capone's career.

Federal agents raided Capone's bootlegging operations. And Treasury Department accountants led by Frank J. Wilson traced his intricately concealed financial affairs, compiling evidence of huge profits on which he had never paid income tax. For this he was sentenced to 10 years in prison (plus another year for contempt).

When Capone was released, Prohibition had been repealed and his day was done. He died in 1947.

Photographed at the time of his contempt trial in February 1931, Al Capone was a beefy 250-pound racketeer who had just passed his 32nd birthday, but had a lifetime of crime behind him and had earned the title Public Enemy No. 1.

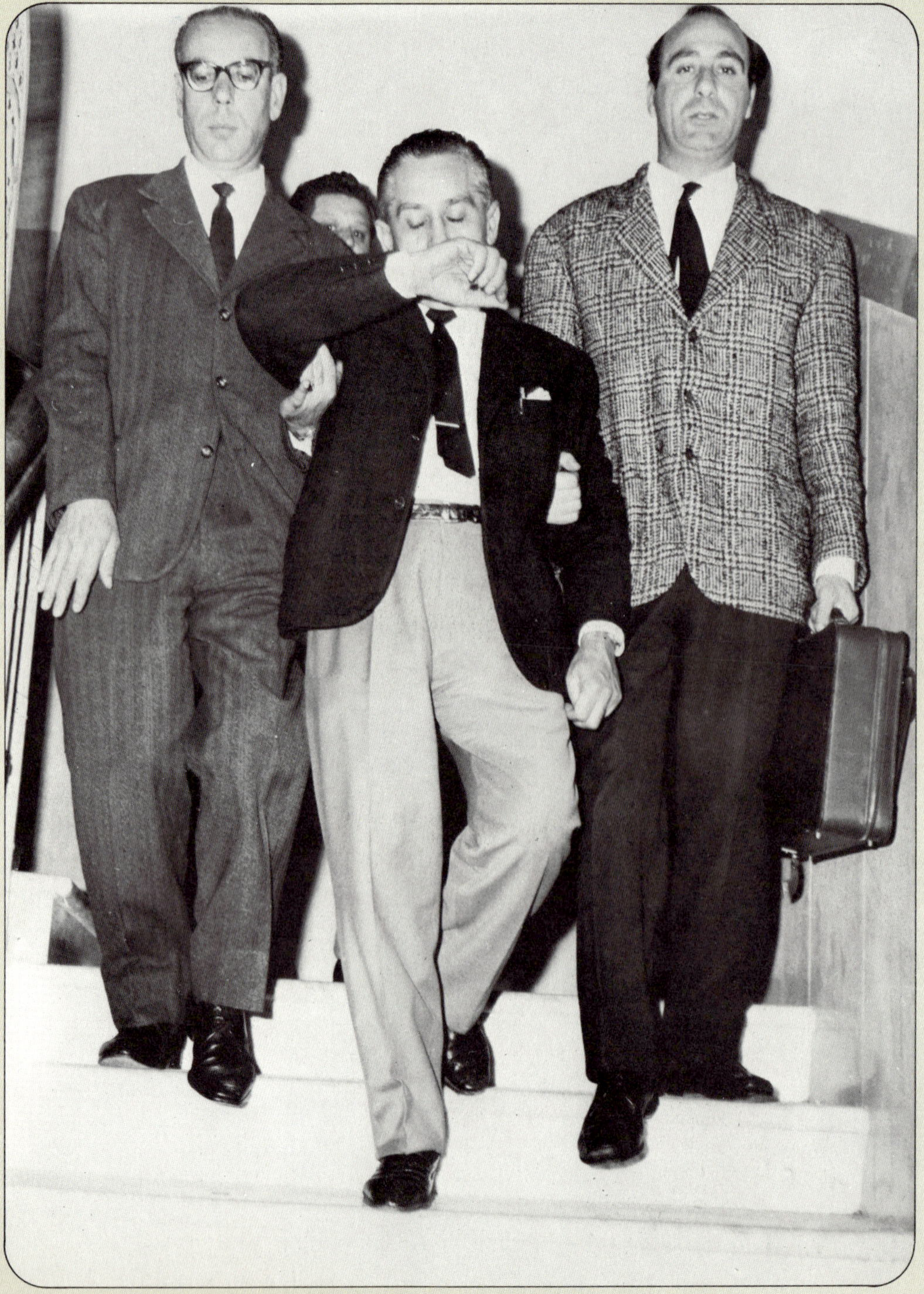

White-Collar Crooks

4

When most people worry about crime, they think about being mugged in the street or burglarized at home. Yet a far more pervasive and, in many ways, more pernicious kind of crime gets scant attention—indeed it is often snickered at. This is white-collar crime: the betrayal of trust by people who are generally regarded as honest citizens in the ordinary course of their lives. White-collar criminals are the "best people": respectable, rarely impoverished and often rich, in many instances among the most powerful and prestigious personages of their society. They lie, steal and cheat.

The economic cost of such activity is astounding; according to one American estimate it is almost a thousand times greater than the loss incurred in bank robberies. The potential for physical harm posed by the deliberate adulterations of food or medicine or cheating on design or manufacturing can be more dangerous than the threat presented by a gun-wielding robber. And perhaps worst of all, white-collar crime corrupts the social organization that enables people to live together peaceably. There are officials, like the Italian customs officer under arrest at left, who accept bribes, corporations that make secret, illegal campaign contributions in order to influence elections, and legislators who sell their influence.

In the end, such behavior corrodes the moral climate of society by providing ordinary criminals—those who commit crimes of violence and other visible offenses—with a convenient excuse for their own wrongdoing. Knowing that businessmen, doctors, judges and lawmakers break the law, the ordinary criminal finds it easy to ask, "If *they* are doing it, why shouldn't I?"

It was not until 1940 that the term white-collar crime was coined by sociologist Edwin H. Sutherland. But such antisocial behavior itself goes back much further. A family prominent in the construction trade in Ancient Greece, the Alcmaeonids, won a contract to build a temple of solid marble but substituted marble-veneer over cheaper stone. In 17th Century England, Sir Francis Bacon sanctimoniously pressed his fellow judges to keep the bench "without scandal and corruption," yet he himself was imprisoned because he extorted bribes—sometimes from litigants on both sides of the same case—while he was the highest judicial officer of his country. In 1833, when President Andrew Jackson was trying to get Congress to pass a bill killing the National Bank, Senator Daniel Webster peddled his influence in blocking passage. In a letter to Nicholas Biddle, the bank's president, Webster warned: "I believe my retainer has not been renewed or *refreshed* as usual. . . . It may be well to send me the usual retainers."

Most white-collar crimes are economic: embezzlements, tax deceits, conspiracies to rig prices. And the most common offense is tax fraud, generally committed by concealing income to avoid paying the government its due.

In France, where outwitting the tax collector is practically a national pastime, nonpayment of taxes cost the government an estimated $11 billion in 1976. The extent to which Frenchmen hide their wealth from the government was indicated by the shock waves that went through the citizenry of Nice in 1976 when the Société Générale bank was looted of about $10 million in valuables and currency in what was dubbed the *fric frac du siècle* ("the heist of the century"). Many wealthy depositors despaired because, to be reimbursed for their losses, they would have to reveal to authorities how much they had stashed away in the bank vault—information that would surely bring demands for unpaid taxes and perhaps even charges of criminal tax evasion.

In Italy, the United Nations reported, citizens managed to avoid paying $12 billion in 1975 taxes. To make up the deficit, the government was forced to adopt stringent austerity measures. Besides cheating on their tax returns, Italians escape payment of taxes by taking money out of the country illegally and depositing it in Swiss banks. According to the United Nations, Italians smuggled $50 billion across the border every year, which was three times the amount their country borrowed abroad to meet its indebtedness. Even in the United States—a country that is remarkable for the comparative honesty of its taxpayers—cheating has a significant effect: by one estimate, the average tax bill might be reduced by 40 per cent if everyone filled out his income-tax return without fudging.

All forms of white-collar crime rob the United States of almost $40 billion every year, according to the Chamber of Commerce. If there were no white-collar crime, almost everything would cost less than it does. A conspiracy among several baking companies to fix bread prices added $35 million to the food budgets of housewives in a single city: Seattle, Washington. Dishonest practices by home-repair contractors may cost Americans as much as one billion dollars every year; in automobile repair, the toll may be $100 million.

Management consultant Norman Jaspan maintains that "losses to American business through embezzlement, missing inventory, manipulation and falsification of records . . . exceed four million dollars a day every working day of the week, every week of the year." Other experts believe that the annual cost of thefts by employees is close to twice the amount lost from crimes like burglary, armed robbery, automobile theft and pickpocketing.

Many experts say that firms lose more goods than cash to dishonest workers. Jaspan estimates that American employees steal a billion dollars worth of merchandise every year. Many pilfer only a few small items for their own use or to give to friends, but others make off with things in huge quantities and then sell them. Ingenious workers have thought up countless ways of getting their loot off company premises without getting caught. A group of Midwest meatpackers swiped choice cuts by strapping them to their bodies. In a Chicago department store that let employees carry out only packages bearing an official stamp, four stock handlers stole the stamp, had a duplicate made, and then walked out with $40,000 in merchandise. A Dallas paper company lost masking tape worth $20,000 when employees dropped cases of it out of factory windows into a heavy growth of weeds.

Dishonest government officials, whose employers are ultimately a nation's citizens, make up a very special group of employees guilty of breeching the confidence placed in them. Since long before John Adams held the opinion that corruption was the very glue of stable government, it has troubled honest citizens. The revelation that bribes had been paid to officials in many nations to induce them to buy aircraft from the Lockheed Aircraft Corporation caused governmental shakeups in Japan, the Netherlands and Belgium, among other countries. In the United States, the accumulation of sordid, petty crimes that came to be known as Watergate forced the expulsion of a President. Although Richard Nixon was not tried for his betrayal of trust in the conduct of his office, his activities were formally adjudged illegal by the New York State Supreme Court.

In 1976 the court disbarred Nixon from the practice of law in New York State after ruling that he had been guilty of serious offenses: obstructing justice by impeding investigation of burglary; interfering with

Financial magnates Cyrus Field, left, and Jay Gould lure investors to some doubtful enterprise. In a Wall Street exposé, Charles and Henry Adams wrote of Gould: "There was a reminiscence of the spider in his nature.... He had not a conception of a moral principle."

THE MOTHS AND THE CANDLE.

The robber barons of laissez faire

In the 19th Century, a dozen or so captains of finance led the revolution that transformed the United States from a mercantile-agrarian society to a nation of factories and big business. Rapacious and unscrupulous, many amassed huge personal fortunes through theft, extortion, blackmail and fraud. With the empire builder's typical arrogance, Cornelius Vanderbilt once asked, "What

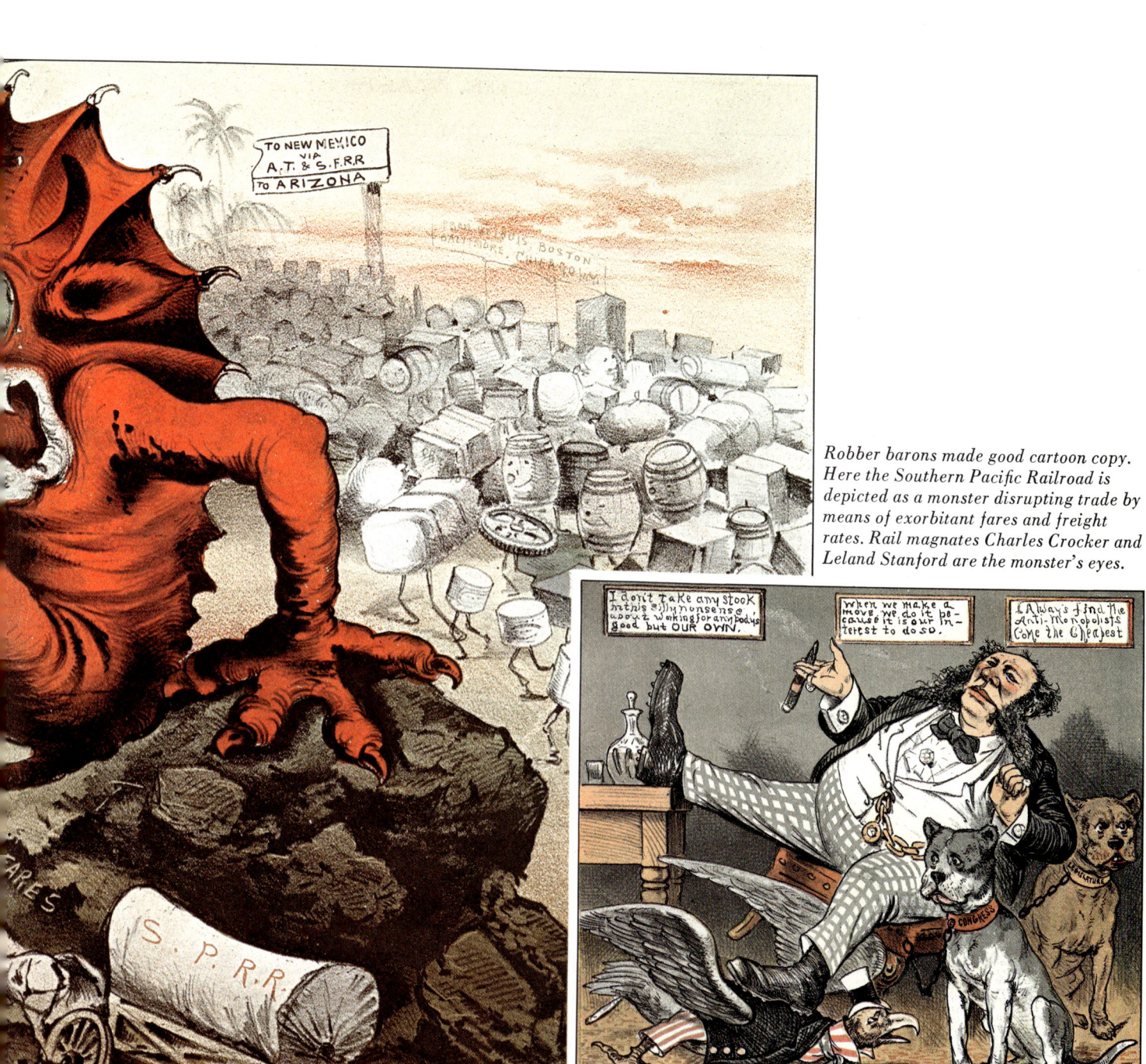

Robber barons made good cartoon copy. Here the Southern Pacific Railroad is depicted as a monster disrupting trade by means of exorbitant fares and freight rates. Rail magnates Charles Crocker and Leland Stanford are the monster's eyes.

"THE PUBLIC BE DAMNED!"

This is William H. Vanderbilt, whom historian Gustavus Myers accused of "dictatorship by money bags." According to Myers, Vanderbilt bribed legislators to change the statutes so that he could tighten his stranglehold on American rail lines.

do I care about the law? Hain't I got the power?"

Few of the economic pirates were ever imprisoned. As social historian Gustavus Myers explains, society "had made money its god," and citizens praised the cleverness of the moguls even while denouncing their knavery. Americans have since become less tolerant of flagrant white-collar crime.

a legal defense in a court case; concealing evidence of crimes committed by his staff; and approving hush-money payments to one of the Watergate conspirators, E. Howard Hunt.

Opportunities for sophisticated white-collar crimes are also created by newly instituted governmental programs, such as an American plan for paying the medical bills of certain poor people.

By billing the government for unnecessary care and for services that had never been rendered, doctors, dentists, druggists and nursing-home operators stole millions of dollars of taxpayers' money. In San Jose, California, a psychiatrist went to jail for treating eight or nine mental patients in a group while billing the state for individual sessions. Some clinics reaped illegal profits from "Ping-Ponging," a term used to mean unnecessarily passing a patient along from specialist to specialist. Other clinics made money from "family ganging." In this swindle, doctors called in whole families for examination whenever one member came in for a checkup. Superfluous X-rays and laboratory tests were ordered and unnecessary medicines prescribed, often under kickback arrangements with pharmacists.

Similarly shady dealings are almost endemic in the business community. Since the days when the Alcmaeonids passed off marble veneer for solid marble, sellers of every imaginable product have defrauded customers with goods that were less than they were made out to be. Only a few years ago scandals in France and Italy shocked European wine drinkers who discovered that what came in the long-necked bottles was not at all what the label claimed.

In 1973, a wine broker named Pierre Bert and 15 wine merchants —among them Cruse et Fils, Frères, the oldest and most prestigious of French wine firms—were convicted of fraud. The house of Cruse had stretched expensive, high-quality red wine from Bordeaux by mixing it with cheap, low-quality reds from the Midi. Bert had sold inexpensive reds as good Bordeaux, for a windfall profit of $800,000. He had also added white wine to inferior Bordeaux reds to cut their astringency, thereby improving the taste. "A little white wine does not harm the quality when there is too much tannin in the red," Bert explained to the court. "But it's not legal," the judge remonstrated. "No, but it's good," Bert came back. He went on to elaborate that it was "the role" of some French wine dealers "to collect bad Bordeaux and improve them." The process, he said, was called "baptism." In the end, Bert was sentenced to spend his nights in prison for six months and to pay a fine of $5,000. Lionel and Ivan Cruse also drew $5,000 fines, plus suspended sentences of 10 months each.

The Cost of White Collar Crimes
(Billions of Dollars)

21 Consumer Fraud, Illegal Competition and Deceptive Practices

7 Embezzlement and Pilferage

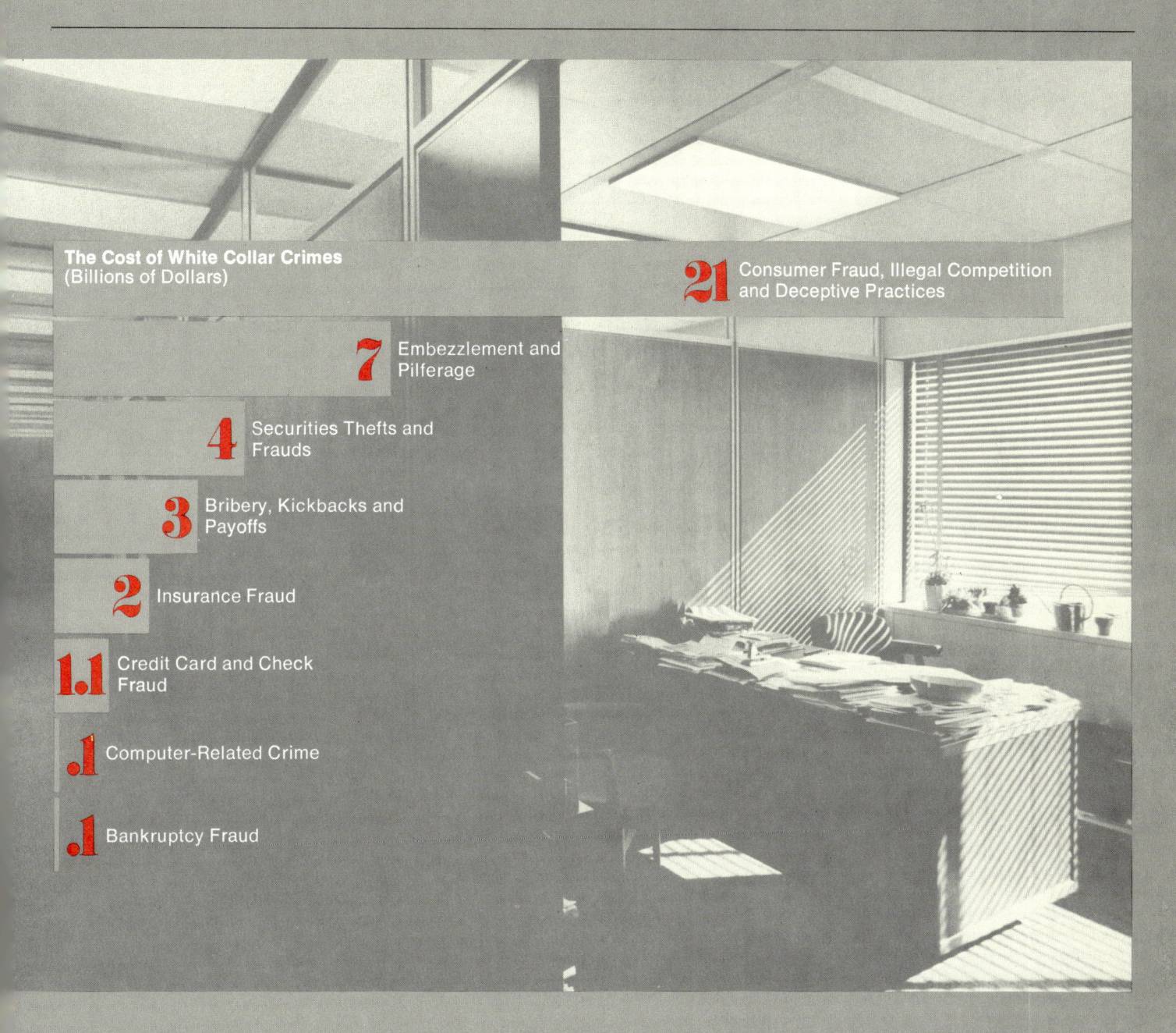

4 Securities Thefts and Frauds

3 Bribery, Kickbacks and Payoffs

2 Insurance Fraud

1.1 Credit Card and Check Fraud

.1 Computer-Related Crime

.1 Bankruptcy Fraud

The high cost of white collar crimes

The "nice" crimes committed by supposedly respectable people are the costliest to society—both in cash and in impact on behavior. The financial loss in the United States alone was nearly $40 billion in 1974. About half that sum, broken down by type of crime in the chart above, resulted from frauds perpetrated on the public by business concerns, the other half from crimes against businesses by individuals.

Such lawlessness is far more costly than ordinary crime. Embezzlement and pilferage, for example, accounted for $4.4 billion more than the losses in the same year from burglary and robbery. Fraud is a factor in the bankruptcies of five U.S. banks a year. A third of all other business failures are caused by employee dishonesty. What cannot be measured are intangible costs—the damage to the institutions of society.

To the presumed mortification of winetasters, who like to think of their palates as highly sensitive, no one ever detected the frauds; Bert testified that he had received not a single complaint from his clients about the quality of the wines he sold them. As Hughes Lawton, the president of the Bordeaux wine merchants association, sorrowfully commented, "A certain mystique has gone."

Italians were not really stunned by their own wine scandal when it erupted in 1968 because most of them already knew that the country's wine industry included manufacturers who not only doctored wine but faked it from the unlikeliest of ingredients. It was estimated during the early 1960s that as much as a third of Italy's "wine" was synthetic. For 10 days in 1967, a squad dubbed the Bacchus police used a helicopter to track deliveries by one of Italy's biggest wine firms, and 10,000 tons of fake wine were seized. By the time the case came to trial, seven wine companies and 174 men and women had been charged with adulterating or faking wine.

One of the recipes they had used was quoted in court. "Crush the pulp and stone of dates, put in a container, mix in hot water, clarify with lead acetate, add sugar, then add acid. Heat to 60 or 70 degrees Centigrade. Let cool immediately and neutralize with potash." Other recipes were even less appetizing. They included no fruit of any kind but called for ammonia, dried oxblood and scum scraped from the bottom of banana boats, among other things. Such formulas prompted Roman wags to revive a familiar tale about an elderly winemaker's legacy to his sons. He called them to his deathbed and confided a bit of secret wisdom to help them after he had gone: "Si fa anche con l'uva" ("You can also make it with grapes").

The wine frauds might be considered amusing; no one was harmed by the synthetic drinks except in his pocketbook. But other adulterations-for-profit are not funny at all; the omission of essential ingredients or the inclusion of inappropriate ones can endanger the health of people who use the products. One of the most outrageous cases of this kind involved the common household remedy ipecac. It is an emetic, a medicine long used to induce vomiting. Many parents routinely keep it in their medicine cabinets, confident that it will save the life of a child who happens to swallow a poison.

During the 1960s, many American parents discovered to their dismay that the syrup they had so trustingly bought to use should a child happen to take poison did not cause vomiting. The Dr. Madis Laboratories of Hackensack, New Jersey, had done something no ordinary consumer could know about: it had substituted ephedrine for two essential ingredients, emeteine and cephaeline. For an economy-minded manufacturer, ephedrine has the advantage of costing only 1/30 as much as the other two chemicals. For a poisoned child, ephedrine has a potentially lethal disadvantage: it possesses no emetic qualities whatever. As psychiatrist Willard Gaylin indignantly wrote, "Dr. Valdemar H. Madis, a Ph.D. in chemistry and a man with long experience in botanical drug manufacture, could not possibly have been unaware of the consequences of his act. He certainly was in a position to know the nature of the adulteration and its effects."

The motives that drove the leader of a great nation to conspire with burglars are impossible to fathom, of course. Yet they may have had much in common with the explanation that seems to apply to much white-collar crime. It is undertaken for special, frequently subtle reasons. Unlike professional crime, it is subsidiary to the normal everyday routine and not the principal activity of life. Unlike most amateur crime, it is reasoned and premeditated, not commonly a response to an emotional drive or an infrequent opportunity for illegal gain. In most cases, white-collar crime seems to be committed to protect an existing way of life, to cope with an overwhelmingly threatening problem that apparently can be solved in no other way.

This view emerges from one of the few sociological studies made of white-collar criminals. In 1953, Donald Cressey reported the findings from interviews with 133 convicted embezzlers. With only a few exceptions, each had been faced with a serious financial problem that he was ashamed to share with anyone because it was the result of his own moral weakness, or bad judgment. Feeling humiliated, each had avoided legitimate loan sources and settled on embezzlement as an easy—in fact, the only—solution.

Cressey cited several cases to illustrate his concept of the unsharable problem. A bank cashier who had siphoned off $25,000 in bank funds over a 10-year period told the sociologist: "I had too much false pride.... Everything that came along I gave to it, and if my friends wanted to borrow $5 or $10, I always gave it to them, and sometimes I knew I never would get it back. I just didn't want folks to think I didn't have money to give, that I wasn't a good sport, that I didn't have anything." He concluded, "If I'd have had guts enough to refuse some of that, I wouldn't be here."

Another bank employee told his fiancée that he earned more than he really did, and he never mustered the courage to tell her the truth. A bookkeeper married a divorcée with three children and two indigent parents, ignoring the warning of his own family that he did not earn enough money to support so many people. Unexpectedly, he was forced to take a drastic reduction in his already low salary, and one of his stepchildren developed an illness requiring costly medical care. The unfortunate bookkeeper could not bear to let his relatives know that their predictions had come true.

Gambling losses are an almost classic factor in embezzlement. A bank teller spent as much as $30,000 a day betting on horse races and other sports events, meanwhile supporting his wife and two children on his $11,000-a-year salary. To maintain this activity he embezzled $1.5 million over a three-year period. "Not one penny went to anything but gambling," he told a reporter after he got out of prison. "I took two lie detector tests when I was arrested, and I think I convinced everyone that I didn't bury any of the money."

Like many modern embezzlers, this one drew money from depositors' accounts by using the bank's computer. When he knew an account would come under scrutiny because interest was due on it, he made up what he had stolen, at least on the computer printout, by transferring funds from other accounts. The process was nerve-racking. "Toward the end," he said, "I was juggling 50 accounts at a time. I was a nervous wreck. It was a relief when they caught me."

In many instances personal financial gain is not the direct motive for white-collar crime. One embezzler, the president of a small-town bank, gained no financial advantage for himself from misappropriating his institution's funds. He conducted his illegal activities in order to help other people. He accommodated many local businessmen by agreeing to make shaky loans and honoring large overdrafts. A grocer explained that when a depositor did not have enough money to cover a check he had written, the banker would "just telephone and say he was putting the check through, anyway. 'You owe me $200 like you owe any other bill,' he'd say. 'Pay me when you get it.'"

Although most depositors did pay up, some did not, and the official began manipulating bank records to conceal the fact that the bank had more liabilities that it had assets. He worked long hours. He got to his office at 7:30 a.m., stayed at his desk to eat the lunch of milk and a fried-egg sandwich that he brought from home every morning, and worked until late most evenings. One day, he found state bank examiners waiting for him when he arrived at work. Usually, he knew in advance when they were due and had the chance to hide incriminating records. This time he was taken by surprise. "You're going to find things in a hell of a shape," he told the examiners. So they did. A local paper firm was overdrawn by about $433,000, a hotel by $225,000. In all, the shortages totaled $1.4 million.

The banker said he had done it all for the local community. Indeed, he was idolized there. After his arrest the town's leading citizens got up a petition asserting that it "is a finer place to live in because of his progressive and unselfish leadership." They also wrote him a letter affirming the "unique affection and regard that we hold for you." One commentator observed that this man had been trying to play God by making people dependent on him and thus everlastingly grateful to him. His embezzlements increased not his fortune but his ego.

A somewhat similar need to sustain or amplify a sense of importance seems to have impelled the participants—all respected, well-paid executives—in the biggest white-collar crime yet prosecuted in the United States. Again, none of the offenders gained a direct financial benefit per-

In 1974, several French wine merchants were convicted of doctoring and mislabeling wine. Among them were cousins Lionel and Ivan Cruse, shown at left at a tasting table in a Bordeaux winery. The Cruses, officers in the 155-year-old firm of Cruse et Fils Frères, drew fines and suspended sentences.

sonally; their actions illegally increased the profits of their corporate employers and aided the men's careers.

In 1961, 29 companies and 45 of their executives were found guilty of conspiring to rig prices and divide up the market for $1.75 billion worth of heavy electrical equipment—circuit breakers, transformers, turbines and the like—every year. Such a cartel agreement is legal in many countries, but in the United States it has been a crime punishable by fines and imprisonment since the end of the 19th Century. The firms included the giants of the electrical industry. Among the defendants were church deacons, the president of a local chamber of commerce, a bank director and the organizer of a Little League baseball team. Despite their eminent respectability, the men had committed acts that were, in the words of sociologist Gilbert Geis, "flagrant, criminal offenses, patently in contradiction to the letter and the spirit of the Sherman Antitrust Act of 1890, which forbade price-fixing arrangements as restraints upon free trade."

When the case came to trial, one of the defendants testified, "I didn't expect to get caught and I went to great lengths to conceal my activities so that I wouldn't get caught." So did all the conspirators. They often used public telephones to communicate with one another and referred to each company by a code number. "This is Bob, what is 7's bid?" one conspirator would ask another as they conspired to set a common price. Planning the face-to-face meetings that they held every two weeks or so, executives talked about the roster of those scheduled to be present as the "Christmas card list" and about the meeting itself as "choir practice." Gatherings were held either in out-of-the-way locations or at trade association conferences, where no one would find the men's presence together suspicious. Even so, they avoided social contact and took the precaution of forgoing the breakfast companionship of fellow conspirators staying in the same hotel.

This gangster-like secrecy was a symptom of the conspirators' unease. Some tried to avoid participation. At one point, when the cartel agreements were to be renewed after a temporary suspension, a manager for the largest company tried to resist, but he eventually gave in to pressure from other divisional general managers. A year later he was promoted out of the job and replaced by a man who was told he held the position "at risk" for two years. If he succeeded, he would become vice president; if he failed, he was out of work.

When the case finally broke, one company began planning a two-part defense for its upper echelon: the conspirators were acting without the encouragement or even the knowledge of the chairman, the pres-

continued on page 128

Flanked by his attorney (left) and his prosecutor, broker Richard Whitney appears in court on a grand larceny charge. He admitted that he had "authorized the unlawful pledge of the securities of other persons" as collateral for personal loans. "I fully realize that certain of my actions have been wrong," Whitney said.

From Harvard to Sing Sing

Richard Whitney was the scion of a prosperous and patrician Massachusetts family. He studied at one of America's most prestigious boys' schools, Groton, where he captained the baseball team, and at Harvard, where he rowed on the varsity crew and was invited to join the exclusive Porcellian Club.

Acquiring both a New York townhouse and a New Jersey estate, Whitney raised cattle and horses and rode to hounds with his beautiful wife. He bought a seat on the New York Stock Exchange, served five terms as its president, and set up a brokerage firm.

But by 1933, Whitney was experiencing some personal financial troubles. Hoping to extricate himself, he organized Distilled Liquors Corporation, a company that manufactured applejack. Unfortunately, not many people cared to drink applejack, and Distilled Liquors, along with some other Whitney ventures, went rapidly downhill. In a futile effort to save his businesses, Whitney dipped into assets entrusted to him by others.

In 1938, his brokerage firm was suddenly forced into bankruptcy and Whitney was arrested. He was prosecuted only for embezzling $214,000 from his father-in-law's estate and from the New York Yacht Club, of which he had been treasurer. But his debts amounted to more than five million dollars. Eventually, his relatives repaid every penny.

In 1932, N.Y.U. awarded Whitney an honorary degree and said his career had "nationwide significance."

The Essex Fox Hounds Hunt meets on Richard Whitney's 495-acre New Jersey estate, one of two residences. Maintaining both cost as much as $5,000 a month even during the Great Depression. Six months before Whitney's arrest, his deteriorating financial situation had led him to mortgage his country house for $300,000.

Whitney enters Sing Sing Prison, where he served 40 months. Walter Bromberg, a court-appointed psychiatrist, noted Whitney's "unconscious feeling of omnipotence": although the broker had known his financial dealings were illegal, he had never once imagined that he might get into trouble with the law.

ident and the other top executives. They had violated a written directive on compliance with the antitrust laws (this document was thought by many in the company to be window dressing that, in practice, was to be ignored) and were therefore liable to corporate punishment. But it came out that the cheating was company-wide; in all, 19 cartels had been operating. So top management was in the awkward position of trying to absolve the company itself while dozens of top managers were being implicated in the conspiracy.

Seven executives in the "electrical conspiracy" were sent to prison. One of them took a revealingly dim view of the fact that his corporate employer docked his pay by $11,000 while he was behind bars. "I got, frankly, got madder than hell," he later told an investigating committee. His outlook is common, for these presumably respectable lawbreakers rarely think of themselves as "real criminals," at least not in the sense that robbers and housebreakers are criminals.

Cressey found that embezzlers rationalized their behavior, telling themselves that they were not stealing but just "borrowing" and would eventually pay back whatever sums they had taken. John Spencer, a British criminologist who made a study of 30 imprisoned white-collar offenders in England, discovered that many men convicted of business frauds also excused themselves readily. "We were just careless—doing what everyone else in business does—but we were unlucky," one said. Norman Jaspan described an embezzler whose idea of the seriousness of her conduct was so out of proportion that although she had stolen $27,000, her first reaction after being caught was to ask, "Is this going to cost me my job?"

Most law-abiding citizens in the West also consider white-collar crime not too serious. Many are blind to it because its social costs are not apparent. Many others are ambivalent, unsure it is truly blameworthy. Some citizens are almost admiring. That attitude is reflected in the old saying, "If you steal a loaf of bread you get a year in jail, but if you steal a railroad you get into the Social Register." Perhaps the commonest response is sympathy. "On the bright side for me personally," one of the electrical conspirators said, have been "the letters and calls from people all over the country, the community, the shops and offices here, expressing confidence in me and support."

This ambiguity in the public attitude toward white-collar crime may stem from the honest person's awareness that given an opportunity, he, too, might find himself unable to resist temptation. However, there is also a cultural basis for such a tendency toward tolerance. What is legal and what is illegal changes sharply and confusingly from time to time and place to place.

In business dealings especially, society once took the position that it was up to people to look after their own interests; if they failed to do so, too bad for them. This situation continues in some parts of the world. Only recently in certain countries has the slogan *caveat emptor* (let the buyer beware) given way to *caveat vendor* (let the seller beware). English courts of the 13th Century provided no recourse for a person who came to grief because he had trusted the word of a liar. As late as the 18th Century, a British chief justice posed this rhetorical question: "When A got money from B by pretending that C had sent for it, shall we indict one man for making a fool of another?" At that time, fraud was looked on as "mere private cheating"; English law did not penalize it until 1757.

The United States had no laws regulating the economic shenanigans of industrial tycoons until late in the 19th century. Before that, almost anything went. Given that climate of opinion, the 19th Century Robber Barons got away with their rapacity *(page 117)*, although there is no question that they violated laws even then on the books. In a battle to purchase a controlling interest in the Harlem Railroad, competitors Cornelius Vanderbilt and Daniel Drew each bribed every alderman in New York City and some state legislators, too. Vanderbilt went his rival one better. He bribed a judge, thus persuading him to issue an injunction that prevented the directors of one railroad from repaying a loan to Drew, forcing a settlement. Questioned about his business tactics, Vanderbilt responded, "You don't suppose you can run a railroad in accordance with the statutes, do you?"

Perhaps because Western society cannot make up its mind about white-collar crime, adequate laws and techniques to control it are rare. Judges tend to be lenient with offenders. Sociologist Gilbert Geis calls the two-million-dollar fines in the electrical case "negligible," and points out that, for one company, a "half-million dollar loss was no more unsettling than a $3 parking fine would be to a man with an income of $175,000 a year." As for 17 American corporations convicted of making illegal political contributions, they were fined an average of only $7,000 each. Since they earned $77,000 a minute, each could square its account with society in just six seconds.

When a California court convicted eight corporate executives of price fixing, the judge imposed neither prison terms nor fines, but ordered each defendant to give a dozen speeches on his crime to business groups. That is not the kind of sentence meted out to conventional offenders. It

Chapter 4

Businessmen in Japan demand an investigation of charges that Lockheed Aircraft Corporation bribed Japanese officials to get them to buy planes from the American company. The charges created a political crisis in Japan.

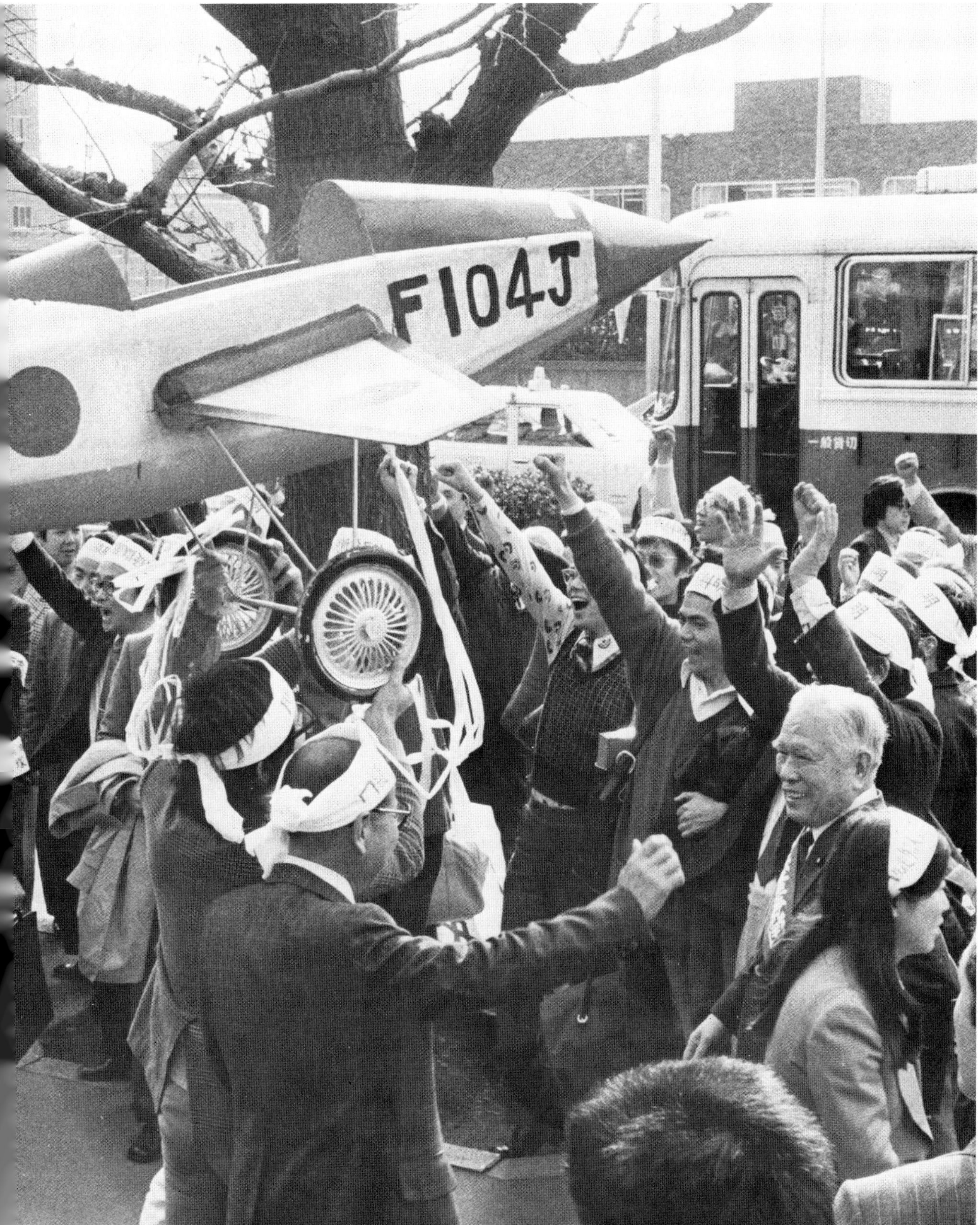
F104J
一般貸切

calls to mind a cartoon that shows a "respectable" criminal standing in court before a stern judge who is telling him, "Warrington Trently, this court has found you guilty of price-fixing, bribing a government official, and conspiring to act in restraint of trade. I sentence you to six months in jail, suspended. You will now step forward for the ceremonial tapping of the wrist."

In non-Western societies, the public has been less tolerant of shady conduct by people of high status, and courts are not so lenient. The Japanese were incensed when it became known that the Marubeni Corporation had accepted bribes from Lockheed to promote the sale of its airplanes in Japan. Local governments canceled millions of dollars in contracts with Marubeni because to them the firm was tainted. Some wives of Marubeni employees began to do their shopping at night so they would not have to face the cold stares of their neighbors. Children whose fathers worked for "the bad, bad company" were jeered at and shamed by other youngsters. One employee said that schoolmates had nicknamed his son Lockheed. Another said his son's teacher had put up a large picture of a Marubeni executive in school and captioned it "dangerous villain." And an outraged young actor ceremonially committed suicide over the case—he deliberately crashed an airplane into the home of a politically powerful lobbyist who had recently been implicated in the Lockheed bribery.

Why the Japanese, almost alone among industrialized peoples, so harshly condemn white-collar crimes, is unclear. Several factors may be involved. For one thing, the tradition of *shuskin koyo*—lifetime employment—which in ordinary times guaranteed not only a permanent job but regular raises and advancement, made each employee a member of a corporate family. As a result, Japanese identify personally with business organizations to a degree unknown in the West.

Even when being introduced socially, a Japanese is likely to link himself with his employer—"I'm Marubeni's Ito." The achievements of the company reflect honor on the employee; in turn its transgressions bring personal disgrace to him. Thus crimes that might be winked at in the West because they were committed for or against a big organization —embezzlement, bribes—are seen in Japan to be individual actions, as reprehensible as the burglary of a home. And everyone connected with the offender is condemned.

The Japanese may also be shocked by white-collar crime because it has become relatively rare in their country. According to official statistics, the rates have decreased sharply. The number of embezzlements dropped by about 55 per cent between 1960 and 1970 and the fraud

Ralph Nader, the aggressively articulate champion of basic consumer rights in the United States, testifies at a 1971 Congressional hearing.

An abrasive crusader for the consumer

When Ralph Nader, the American son of a Lebanese immigrant, got out of Harvard Law School in 1958, he believed there were too many lawyers looking after corporate interests and too few who cared about consumers. Since then he has been waging an all-out battle against wrong-doing in the world of big business. Nader is not a man to mince words; he says straight out that he thinks many executives belong in jail. "Not since the robber-baron era have so many major companies and their officials been found to have violated the law," Nader charged.

As a result of his exposés of corporate crime and his tireless consumer advocacy, officials at all levels of U.S. government bear down harder on law-breakers in business and industry.

Nader is also largely responsible for the passage of several stringent laws designed to protect the public against a wide variety of hazards. For example, the Motor Vehicle Safety Act of 1966 requires automobile manufacturers to build cars incorporating certain safety features. The Wholesome Meat Act of 1967, drawn up after inspection revealed that some packing plants were filthy and rodent-infested, ordered the states to upgrade their standards of cleanliness. Other Nader-inspired legislation deals with radiation hazards and with the safety of mining and many other occupations.

cases by 30 per cent. Whether the statistical decline in known cases accurately reflects a like decline in the total number of such occurrences is impossible to tell. The Lockheed scandal drew from several Japanese businessmen the comment that similar bribery is common and seldom uncovered; the disgrace, they suggested, is less in committing the crime than in being caught at it.

Aside from Japan, the only major nations that seem—officially at least—to take white-collar crime deadly seriously are the Communist countries, particularly China and the U.S.S.R. Both punish offenders very severely.

In 1961 and 1962, the Soviet Union made bribery, embezzlement and other so-called economic crimes capital offenses. In a four-year period, Soviet courts sentenced an estimated 200 people to death for these white-collar crimes. One of that number, T. Chkekheidze, chief engineer in a candy factory, was convicted of heading a ring that embezzled $76,000 worth of ingredients by siphoning off cognac, using treacle instead of honey and substituting margarine for butter. Another white-collar criminal executed by the Soviets was a government wheat-mill inspector who stole thousands of tons of flour and covered up the loss by juggling the books and by adding moisture to the remaining flour to make it weigh more. Over a decade later, five canning-factory officials were sentenced to execution by a firing squad for selling the government nonexistent vegetables in a $12 million fraud.

Despite the savage penalties, such crimes are very common in the U.S.S.R. Statistics are kept secret, but economic corruption has been called Russia's most persistent crime problem. From the unprivileged to the elite, operating *na levo* ("on the left") seems to be a way of life. Government limousines are used as gypsy cabs, paper marriages are arranged to get legal-residency documents for scarce apartments, factory workers pocket consumer goods and spare parts for resale outside, farmers feed state grain to their privately owned livestock.

Such cheating extends to the very highest levels of the government. Russia's most prominent woman official, Yekaterina A. Furtseva, Minister of Culture, was officially reprimanded by the Communist Party for building a luxury dacha outside Moscow with $170,000 worth of state building materials, which she acquired at a bargain rate. She was made to repay a large sum and, apparently as a result of the scandal, was passed over as a candidate for the Supreme Soviet. Reportedly only the personal intervention of Premier Leonid Brezhnev saved her from being dropped as a cabinet minister.

The paradox of occasional brutal punishment alongside a general broad tolerance may be explained by the fact that white-collar crimes are especially embarrassing in a Communist society. Diverting state goods for private profit is a "shameful survival of the past," rendering invalid a staggering amount of planning, and it makes the government lash out in retaliation. "But people still take risks because the opportunities are there," a Russian woman explained. Many Russians feel that there is less social stigma attached to commercial thievery in their country than there is in capitalist nations because all means of production are state owned. "We have two economies—state and private," one man told a reporter. "The state economy produces and the private economy consumes. It's natural, because you can't get along otherwise. Whoever steals, lives better."

While no one in the West agrees with the Communist belief that white-collar criminals deserve to die, many behavioral experts think that they are often treated too gently. Psychoanalyst Willard Gaylin, for one, commented that Madis's sentence in the ipecac case was too light, perhaps because it was based on the defendant's seeming respectability. But, Gaylin said, "It is a peculiar definition of respectability that excludes the source of the money with which such respectability is bought. If ever a case for prison time can be made, it would seem that this is it. Six months in a penitentiary would have been hard service for a 65-year-old man. But it would have put the white-collar community on notice that there are no privileged under the law."

Sociologist Edwin Schur noted that in the United States, at least, white-collar crime is "grossly underreported and underprosecuted. Americans have become alarmingly inured to the practice of fraud.... That 'respectable crime' has been an object of selective inattention in American life is itself one of the major crimes of our society."

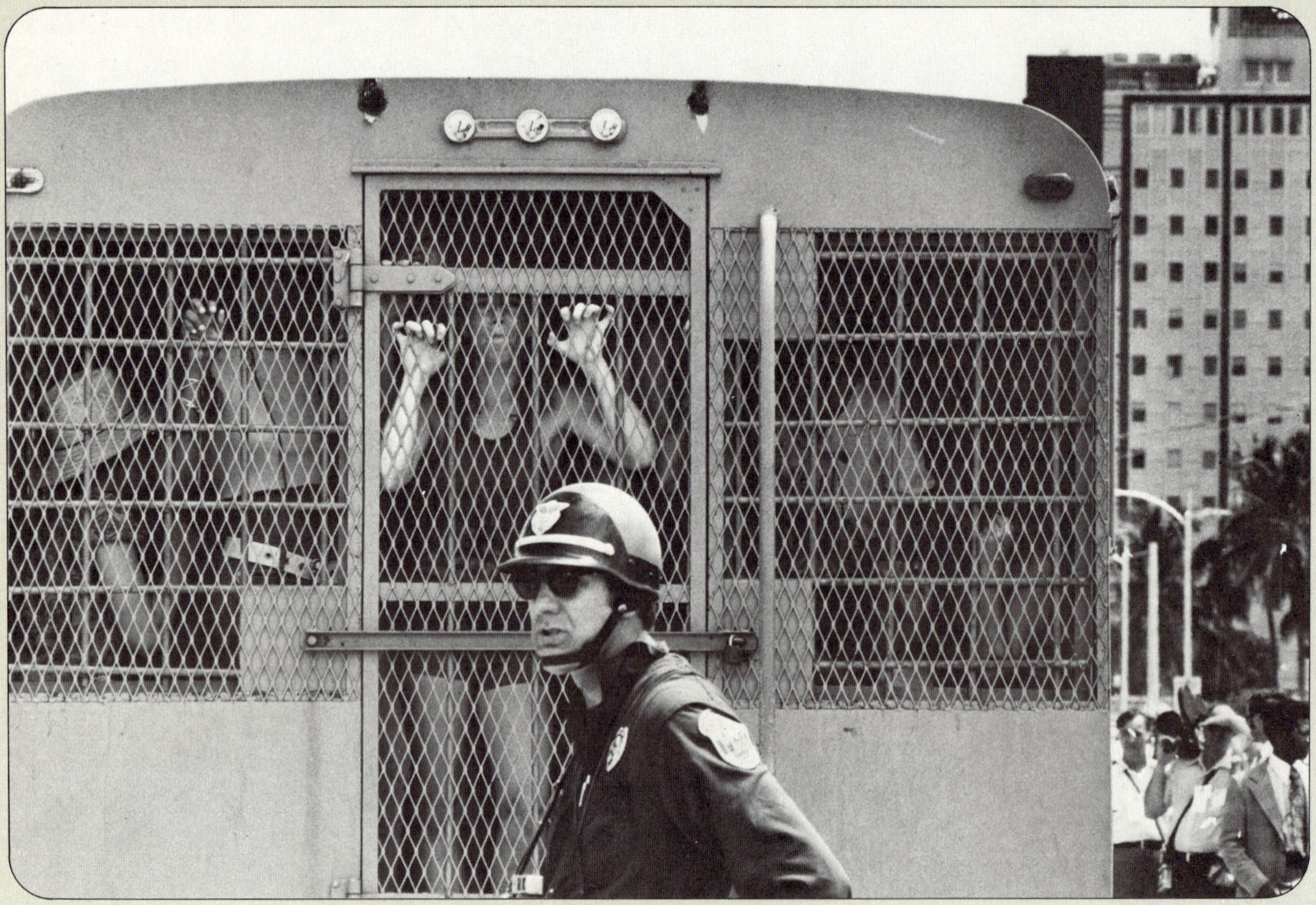

The Justice System

5

Richie the Pawnbroker had been running a successful fencing operation for a year: he and his aides had managed to buy $700,000 worth of stolen merchandise for $45,000. They decided it was time for a party, and invitations went out, by letter, telephone and word of mouth, to 140 thieves who had supplied loot ranging from stolen checks, credit cards and negotiable bonds to jewelry, an electrocardiograph and 700 brand-new brassieres. The thieves were promised liquor, girls and party favors in the form of new $100 bills, one for every guest. Besides, they would get a chance to meet the local Mafia chieftain. "No guns, positively no guns," Richie warned his guests in advance. "Mr. Big don't like guns. And I don't want no fights over the dames."

Taxis picked up the guests and took them to an isolated warehouse where, as Richie's partner Joey said, "There ain't goin' to be no beefs about the noise." The atmosphere was festive. Sandwiches and liquor had been set out. Richie and his fellow fences wore dinner jackets. Music throbbed from a jukebox, and psychedelic lights pulsed and swirled.

A surprise greeted guests as they entered. Ten men carrying drawn guns and wearing jackets emblazoned with the word police announced, "You are under arrest." Two of the guests impatiently asked when the joke would be over so they could get on with the party. "This *is* the party," Richie the Pawnbroker told them. He was, in reality, Detective Richard Ledda of the New York City Police Department, and his party was the climax of an imaginative police scheme, since copied in many places, for rounding up professional thieves.

Such a complexly orchestrated plan for apprehending lawbreakers is a modern wrinkle in society's long-drawn-out attempt to cope with crime. Even the idea of assigning someone to the job of apprehending offenders is relatively new. While laws, and the procedures for enforcing them, are as old as human culture, only in more recent times has the criminal-justice system been compartmentalized into the separate structures that now exist almost everywhere: police, who try to prevent crime and to identify the perpetrators when it occurs; prosecutors, who bring formal charges; courts, which determine whether the charges are justified and, if so, what penalty should be imposed; and prisons, which punish wrongdoers and attempt to prevent them from repeating their offenses.

At every level of the system, officials possess wide discretionary powers. They can ignore or react to certain crimes, arrest one person rather than another, bring charges of greater or lesser seriousness, take into account or brush aside extenuating circumstances and thus impose a light penalty or a harsh one. Yet the goal is to make all persons equal before the law. Freud, echoing sentiments expressed in almost every legal code since Hammurabi, said, "The first requisite of civilization is justice—that is, the assurance that a law once made will not be broken in favor of an individual."

The newest of the distinct units of the modern criminal-justice system is the one that is now at the spearhead of the fight against crime: the police. It was not until 1829 that the first uniform-wearing force was established, in London, by Sir Robert Peel (his men were initially called peelers, after his last name, and only later became bobbies, after his first). From the beginning, the social purpose of these newly created community guardians was seen to be new. "It should be understood," said a statement issued by the first commissioner of the force, "that the principal object to be attained is *the prevention of crime*. To this great end every effort of the police is to be directed. The security of persons and property, the preservation of public tranquillity and all the other objects of a Police Establishment will thus be better effected than by the detection and punishment of the offender after he has succeeded in committing the crime."

In their secondary function—detecting crime—the police have pioneered in the application of newly developed technology. Fingerprint identification was adopted by Scotland Yard in 1901, and today techniques of nuclear physics can find infinitesimal traces of gunpowder on a hand that has recently fired a gun. Computers rapidly print out file data on likely suspects, television shows in several countries enlist public assistance in locating lawbreakers *(page 159)*, and instant communications and worldwide police networks can be brought into play against international crooks. By 1976, more than 100 countries belonged to Interpol, short for International Criminal Police Organization. With its headquarters in St. Cloud, France, Interpol has been coordinating the investigative work of its member nations since 1923. Before that, a criminal could be almost certain of escaping punishment if he could simply slip unnoticed out of his own country. No more. "Because of Interpol, there is virtually no place left to hide," said a Scotland Yard official.

Interpol gets busier every year. In 1975, the organization worked on 25,000 cases, about two and one half times the figure for 1970, and in 1975 its radio system transmitted 220,000 messages, an increase of 13 per cent over the earlier year. Officials of the international group keep hands off hijacking cases and other crimes with political implications. They are afraid of alienating a member nation and thus losing its support in the fight against such noncontroversial crimes as counterfeiting, drug trafficking and theft of credit cards and traveler's checks.

One 1969 crime that Interpol helped solve followed a script worthy of a movie thriller. For a while Western Europe was flooded with counterfeit Swiss 100-franc notes. Through Interpol, police in Belgium, Britain, Switzerland and West Germany pooled their information about people found to possess the notes in such large quantities that they could not have acquired them innocently. Three such people were arrested in West Germany, and Swiss police flew in to question them. One of the three suspects, a Swiss, admitted that he was scheduled to fly to Britain to pick up a huge new consignment of phony bills. To prove his *bona fides* to the counterfeiters, he was to hand his British contact a fake franc note marked in a special way.

Armed with this information, Interpol helped Swiss police arrange a rather risky ploy. While the Swiss suspect languished in jail in West Germany, a French-speaking Scotland Yard officer impersonated him. Carrying out the planned mission to Great Britain, the officer succeeded in penetrating the ring of counterfeiters. As a result of his efforts, 25 criminals from four countries were arrested within three months of the time when the first bad franc note came to light. "Without the cooperation through Interpol, the whole thing would have taken much longer and we wouldn't have caught as many of the criminals," said a spokesman for Scotland Yard.

It is only recently that the primary function of police—preventing crime—has benefited from modern science with the application of the new understanding of human behavior. Psychological research, in particular, has shown ways to prevent violence in several kinds of explosive situations.

One such situation is created by family quarrels, which are the major precursors of homicides. Work with families in crisis is one of the most time-consuming and hazardous of all police duties. In New York City, for example, it consumes as many hours as any other single form of police work. In the United States as a whole, one of every five policemen killed on duty dies trying to end a family fight. New York responded by setting up the Family Crisis Intervention Unit made up of policemen specally trained in understanding human behavior and in damping down potentially homicidal anger.

The unit was formed with the help of two psychologists, Morton Bard and Bernard Berkowitz, both of whom had previously worked as active policemen. The two put together a special program of study, including not only formal classroom work but psychodramas enacted by Plays for Living, an organization that utilizes theater as a training tool in the field of mental health. The script for each playlet dramatized a family quarrel a policeman might encounter, carrying the action to a point just short of explosion into violence. From then on, a pair of policemen intervened and, with the actors, tried to extemporize their way to a peaceful resolution of the crisis.

The specially trained officers seek to establish themselves as helpful rather than authoritarian figures. They use some of the techniques of group therapy to uncover the trouble underlying the family's dispute. "We try to make them see their real problems," patrolman John Edmonds explained. "Then we ask them what they're going to do about it." The results of such efforts were so promising that, according to Inspector Neil Behan, the program quickly led to significant changes in the training of police.

Techniques derived from psychology have also been applied to control another kind of dangerous crime: the use of hostages. Some are taken by ordinary criminals to shield escape; others may be seized by a deranged person to prove he can still wield power of a sort; and still others are held by professional terrorists to make a political point *(pages 24-25)* or gain a political advantage.

In the movies, captors and captives are promptly besieged by police, who call in a minister or a member of a criminal's family to bring about a peaceful surrender. In real life, police have discovered, such a ploy is often the spark that ignites smoldering violence. As Frank Bolz, coordinator of New York City's pioneering Hostage Negotiating Team, explained their approach in cases of a suspect holding hostages, "We don't allow his wife or mother or priest to go in there with him. If he got along with his wife, if his mother loved him and if he believed in the church, he wouldn't be where he is."

After the tragedy of the 1972 Munich Olympics, when Arab terrorists took and then murdered 11 Israeli hostages, Detective Harvey Schlossberg of the New York Police Department was assigned to develop psychologically sophisticated methods of resolving hostage crises. Schlossberg was chosen because he had earned a doctorate at the New York Center for Psychoanalytic Training. Eventually, he helped set up the 68-member Hostage Negotiating Team. "Our approach resembles crisis intervention therapy for suicidal people," Schlossberg said. "You try to establish contact with the person, identify with him, find out his problem and get him to look for another solution. By asking the criminal questions, you force him to put his feelings into words. What we're looking for is time until his anxiety maybe abates and the negotiations appear to offer him an alternative course of action. As hours pass, the guy becomes bored, tired, makes mistakes." By contrast, the police negotiators are fresh and alert because they can work in shifts. Under these conditions, hostages can often slip safely away from their captors.

Another advantage of waiting out the criminal is that useful, if bizarre, emotional relationships begin to develop between captor and hostage on the one hand and captor and police on the other. Through

Two salesmen, taking enforcement of the law into their own hands, wrestle with a thief who walked out of their Baltimore shop with a suit of clothes. One of the salesmen holds down the struggling offender's head while the other grips a trouser leg until the police arrive.

Chapter 5

the process of transference, the hostages and the policemen may take on the significance of people who have been important to the criminal in the past. As a result it becomes harder for him to kill his hostages and easier to comply with the requests of the police.

One tactic is to try to reduce the criminal's hostility and build his ego in small ways. The idea is to keep from humiliating him and thus goading him to strike out violently by way of compensation. The police may tell a captor, "That's a good idea," or, "You have a point there." When a deranged New Yorker named Floyd Steele shot his landlord to death and took a five-year-old girl as a hostage, one of Frank Bolz's ploys was to address him as "Mr. Steele" while they chatted through a closed door about such nonviolent topics as geraniums and Steele's life as a gandy dancer, or itinerant railway worker. Under this respectful treatment, Steele relaxed and opened the door a crack. The police then seized the hostage, and Steele surrendered.

Outside the United States, police use similar psychological tactics. They are patient and prudent, and they try hard to create some sort of relationship among terrorists, hostages and lawmen. However, they place somewhat less emphasis on the safety of the captives than New York policemen do. Bolz emphasized that "the life of the hostage is the most important thing; apprehension of the criminal or terrorist is secondary." By contrast, Sir Robert Mark, chief of police in London, said, "To be perfectly blunt about it, we are prepared to sacrifice the life of the hostages if it comes to that." And the Israelis, of course, have been willing to accept grave risks in order to free hostages in defiance of terrorists, as they demonstrated in the daring rescue of 103 captives from the airport at Entebbe, Uganda, in 1976.

The two main police functions, preventing crime and capturing criminals, merge in hostage situations. In most other instances, taking a criminal into custody is an entirely separate operation, and a difficult one, for ordinarily the police must first figure out who he is. In this task the science of human behavior has aided more often than not in a negative way, by demonstrating the fallacies in old methods.

Eyewitness accounts, for example, have been the foundation of criminal trials for centuries. Only in recent times has their unreliability been established as experiment after experiment showed that witnesses misremember what they have seen and, because of unconscious bias, twist their recollections. In recent tests at California State University, psychologist Robert Buckhout and his colleagues staged a classroom assault on a professor. Seven weeks later they asked students to scrutinize photographs of six people and identify the "guilty" person. Sixty per

142

continued on page 147

Following the example of their instructor (front row, left), Japanese police cadets sit cross legged and meditate before a martial-arts class. Meditation helps the student focus his mental energy upon the training and—so the Japanese believe—increases his powers of concentration.

Japan's well-rounded police

With worldwide crime rates steadily rising, Japan is apparently unique: it has managed to reduce criminal activity. The incidence of violent crimes—homicide, rape, armed robbery and assault—declined by an astonishing one third between 1950 and 1975. Social scientists attribute part of the decline to the deep-seated Japanese reverence for authority, reflected in a widespread public support for law-enforcement efforts. Credit is also given to the Japanese policeman, whose careful, rigorous training prepares him to be an active, highly esteemed member of the community.

At Tokyo's Police Academy *(above and overleaf)* cadets study such familiar subjects as crime detection, law and community relations. They also learn Japanese martial arts such as *kendo*—a form of sword fighting—and judo. Peculiar to Japanese academies, however, is *joso kyoiku*—literally, "upper-crust education"—which includes flower arranging, calligraphy, performing the tea ceremony and chanting ancient poetry. Such character-building courses, an instructor explained, help counteract the "brutalizing" nature of police work.

Along with its psychological benefits, the *joso kyoiku* training also identifies a police officer with the most respected cultural and intellectual pursuits in Japan—thus elevating his status in the eyes of his countrymen. Many officers ultimately live in the neighborhoods that they police, and the Japanese policeman is generally welcomed into a community both as a skilled enforcer of the law and as a cultured neighbor.

143

Protected by thick cotton tunics, bamboo armor and steel-grill helmets, police recruits flail at each other with wooden swords during a kendo class. Mastery of such martial arts earns an officer his fellow citizens' respect—and also aids him in overpowering resistant suspects.

Police recruits are introduced to the esthetics of flower arranging. They are required to wear dress uniforms during these classes, which are considered to build character as well as to acquaint a policeman with honored Japanese cultural traditions.

An instructor inspects fingernails before a class in aikido, a form of judo-like fighting that is taught to women police recruits and is used only for defense.

Making his daily rounds in Tokyo, a police officer admires a dwarf tree, or bonsai, grown by an elderly gardener. Constant personal involvement with the interests of varied neighbors enables the Japanese policeman to enforce the law in an atmosphere of mutual respect.

cent of the witnesses, among them the victim of the attack, picked out the wrong man. A fourth of the mistaken witnesses chose someone they had seen when the incident took place, but he had been an innocent bystander. In another experiment, Harvard psychologist Gordon Allport showed subjects a drawing of a scene in which the central figures were a black man clad in a business suit and a white man wearing work clothes and brandishing a razor. Half the subjects later said it was the black man who carried the razor.

As unreliable as eye-witness testimony is that other staple of the criminal investigation, the confession. Many well-publicized murders lead to false confessions by emotionally disturbed people who perhaps harbor murderous wishes in their unhappy but innocent souls. In nearly all cases, the falsity of such admissions is obvious. The case of Jerome R. is an exception.

In 1952, Jerome was arrested for the murder of the woman he loved, Madeline B. His conviction appeared certain. He had once been a professional photographer; she had been a teacher of music. Both of them drank too much and were probably neurotic, but they were not psychotic. Jerome once described their relationship to a psychiatrist. "We couldn't get along without each other. It was a meeting of minds and bodies." After Madeline's death, a bartender remembered, "They were hard drinkers and sad drinkers, but they weren't mean drinkers. They just sat close together at the end of the bar and looked at each other all the time and didn't talk much. Madeline drank more than he did, and sometimes she would cry and he would put his arm around her and take her home. He sure seemed to be in love with Madeline."

In April of 1952, the couple tried, unsuccessfully, to commit suicide by slashing their wrists. "We couldn't get along in the world and we wanted to escape, that's all," Jerome explained. They made up their minds to try again, and in December, Jerome was found dazed in their gas-filled apartment, while Madeline lay dead in bed. As Jerome explained to the police, he and Madeline had agreed the previous week that he would kill her and then put an end to his own life. They went to bed about midnight, both of them sober. "We just curled up and went to sleep," Jerome told the police. He woke up about three, and he shook Madeline's shoulder gently. "I said, 'This is it, honey.' . . . I kissed her. . . . She said, 'O.K.' . . . I strangled her."

Yet Jerome was freed after an autopsy had been performed on Madeline. "This girl wasn't strangled," the examining surgeon reported. "There isn't any evidence at all that anybody even attempted to strangle her. She died of occlusive coronary arteriosclerosis and acute alcoholism." The surgeon added, "I guess the poor guy just had been planning all those days to kill her and himself one way or another, and maybe had been planning to strangle her without telling her he was going to do it that way, and when he saw she was dead, he thought he *had* strangled her."

The fundamental difficulties that hamper the policeman in performing his job are magnified by his ambiguous position in society. In many places, he is depended on and admired. But he may also be feared and distrusted. Such contradictory attitudes are fostered by the police officer's singular power. Restraints on his use of power are limited and difficult to apply. Abuse is inevitable. Amnesty International, an organization that tries to protect political prisoners, reported in 1974 that police in more than 60 countries torture suspects, and the Social Committee of the United Nations General Assembly has called for adoption of an international code of police ethics.

Custom and law governing police conduct vary from country to country. In Italy, regulations limit the police in the use of guns. French police are not so sharply restricted. In Paris, for instance, each officer has the freedom to exercise his discretion in the use of his semiautomatic pistol, his baton and his leaded cape, which can be swung in crowds with devastating effect, to restore public order.

In Japan, police are no less tough, but they are more subtle. They carry pistols, but they are much more likely to use judo and nonlethal weapons. Japanese police are trained to avoid even this much violence if possible; training includes the tea ceremony, flower arrangement and calligraphy *(pages 143-146)*. This low-key approach to crime control apparently suits the Japanese; public-opinion polls show that the police are widely respected.

The same thing is true in Britain. In one poll, 90 per cent of those questioned said they considered the police helpful, efficient and honest. Traditional British courtesy may be one factor. Michael Banton, professor of sociology at Bristol, observes that when a British police officer reproves someone, he makes it clear that he means nothing personal but is just doing his job. "This impersonality," Banton says, "enables him to behave in a deferential manner to all sorts of people. An officer can come up to a woman who is trying to park her car in a stupid position, salute, inquire 'Can I help you, madam?' and then persuade her to leave it elsewhere." Few Americans would dispute Banton when he adds, "The chances of a British policeman's behaving in an impersonal and deferential manner—of acting solely as the incumbent of a role—are far higher than the chances of an American officer's doing so."

The British officer's reluctance to use force is another. Except under very special circumstances the London bobby goes armed with nothing more lethal than a truncheon. Even that is kept out of sight most of the time. "I have never drawn mine in anger," a typical London constable named Peter Roland Sawyer (or Tom for short) told a journalist a few years ago. "I don't believe in it. It's old-fashioned. We're taught enough self-defense so that if a chap comes at you with a missile or an iron bat, you should be able to handle him. Of course, if a chap comes up and gives you a real solid clout behind the ear, you may think of drawing the stick, but what you actually do is to give him a real solid clout back. Funnily enough, that doesn't cause any rancor. Chummy thinks, well, he's not such a bad bloke."

If he wanted to pay for them himself, Sawyer could carry handcuffs, but he thinks "they're a bit primitive, really." He says that, in fact, "I've never known anybody who carried them. I think you can reason

Posing as Santa Clauses in front of a New York department store, two police decoys take into custody a suspected shoplifter. Police the world over employ the decoy technique to catch criminals red-handed.

with most chaps. If you've caught a fellow and he's particularly aggressive, you just watch him alertly and he won't try to get away."

As for guns, Sawyer said that carrying pistols "would ruin our relationship with the public." He elaborated: "If I suddenly appeared on the beat next week with a nice shiny holster holding a gun, I am sure there would instantly be a wall of animosity between me and all the traders and other people I see and chat with. I would no longer be their friend. I would be set apart."

In America, nearly all policemen carry revolvers. And they use them frequently. A study of 450 policemen in 1966 found that one of every 10 used "improper" or "unnecessary" force. Psychotherapist Arthur Kobler investigated 911 cases of "homicide by legal intervention" that were committed between 1965 and 1969, and he discovered that for every policeman killed while on duty, five civilians had died at the hands of the law. According to Kobler, 25 per cent of the civilians had been unarmed, 25 per cent had been shot in the back, 27 per cent had been committing offenses against property rather than crimes of violence when killed, and 30 per cent had been guilty of nothing at all or, at most, of a traffic violation or other misdemeanor. Police reported that 75 per cent of their civilian victims had been either attacking or fleeing when they were shot, but Kobler expressed skepticism. In many instances there were no civilian witnesses. When civilian bystanders were present, they agreed that policemen had been defending themselves against real danger in only 40 per cent of the cases.

The difficulty of the policeman's lot was summarized by the English lawyer Ben Whittaker. "The public uses the police as a scapegoat for its neurotic attitude toward crime," he said. "Janus-like we have always turned two faces toward a policeman.... We resent him when he enforces the law in our own case, yet demand his dismissal when he does not elsewhere. We offer him bribes, yet denounce his corruption. ... We admire violence, even against society itself, but condemn force by the police on our behalf. We tell the police that they are entitled to information from the public, yet we ostracize informers. We ask for crime to be eradicated, but only by the use of 'sporting' methods."

Once the police have identified and captured a suspect, the next step in the criminal justice process is prosecution, or the bringing of formal charges as a prelude to trial. In most countries, the police themselves bring charges only in minor cases; otherwise this task falls to an official prosecutor.

Accusing a person of breaking the law can have momentous consequences for his future life. Thus the power of the prosecutor is very great. It is not just that he makes the decision to press a case or drop it. In some countries, he can also challenge and perhaps overturn a sentence if he thinks a court has treated an accused person too leniently. And in many systems, the prosecutor determines the specific charge against a defendant and thus, indirectly, the severity of his sentence if he is found guilty.

The case of Gabrielle Russier in France became a notorious example of the power prosecutors can wield. Madame Russier was a dedicated teacher in Marseilles. At 30, she fell in love with one of her 17-year-old students, Christian Rossi, and he with her. The situation is a familiar one in the writings of Racine, Stendahl and Colette, but the real-life outcome was harsher than most writers of fiction imagine.

Christian's parents sued Gabrielle for seducing a minor. She was arrested and jailed for eight weeks to keep her away from the boy. Then, on July 10, 1969, she was tried, found guilty, fined 500 francs and given a suspended sentence of 12 months. Under French law, criminals sentenced to a year or less are automatically pardoned as soon as a new president takes office. Thus Gabrielle could expect that her name would be cleared and that she could go on teaching.

The penalty was too light to suit the public prosecutor. Thirty minutes after the sentence was handed down, he moved for retrial and demanded that Gabrielle be sentenced to 13 months in prison, a period that would prevent a pardon under the amnesty statute. Faced with the prospect of going back to jail, the burden of a lifelong criminal record and the loss of her right to teach, Gabrielle committed suicide. Her story was turned into a movie, *To Die of Love*. Books were written about her. Newspapers pictured her as the victim of a harsh and vengeful criminal-justice system, and a storm of public outrage broke over all of France.

Madame Russier's case is unusual, but instances in which a prosecutor seals a man's fate by determining the charge against him are legion. A prosecutor has considerable leeway. Under certain circumstances, he may either accuse a suspect of a serious crime carrying a heavy penalty, or he may charge a lesser offense for which the law imposes a figurative slap on the wrist. A killing may be called a murder and the penalty may be death, or it may be characterized as manslaughter and lead to a prison sentence of only a few months. A theft may be described as a felony (a grave crime) or a misdemeanor (a fairly minor offense). Statute books spell out the characteristics of different degrees of the same crime, but in practice the distinctions are not always clear-cut; in a particular crime, the facts may lend themselves to several interpretations.

This situation is common in all modern countries, but in the United States it leads to a process rare in other parts of the world, plea bargaining. Before court proceedings begin, the prosecutor and the accused, or his lawyer, enter into negotiations and strike a bargain. The prosecutor agrees to reduce the charge on which the suspect was arrested if the defendant will agree to plead guilty. In Europe, a guilty plea has no practical consequences; the prosecutor must prove his case in court anyway. But in the United States, a plea of guilty ensures conviction without a trial. It seems, then, that plea bargaining is an efficient way of expediting cases. Without it, there would be so many cases to be tried that the American court system could handle only a tiny fraction of them. As it is, about 90 per cent of serious criminal cases in the United States are settled by negotiations out of court.

Prosecutors gain from plea bargaining because they are spared the necessity of arguing a case and the possibility of losing it. Also, suspects may give the prosecutor information about other crimes or agree to testify against other criminals in exchange for leniency. At the same time, guilty defendants like plea bargaining because it assures them the lesser sentence that goes with a lesser charge. In fact, that is one of the main

The complex art of making an arrest

In most democracies, making an arrest is an art requiring judgment, legal knowledge and perceptiveness. Abusive language or unjustified force can provoke an attack on the officer, yet he must act decisively and quickly to prevent flight. A "bad arrest," in which the officer obtains deficient evidence or fails to advise the suspect of his rights, might get the case thrown out of court.

When New York City police officer Alice McCain arrested a man accused of throwing lye at his neighbor, photographer Sepp Seitz, who had been in the police car with her and her partner Detective Charles O'Connor, recorded her skillful handling of the arrest. The procedure is repeated in this basic form for each of the nine million arrests made in the United States yearly.

In her patrol car, police officer McCain records a radio message ordering her to arrest a lye-throwing assailant, and telling her where to look for him.

objections to plea bargaining: in some cases it may permit a murderer to get off almost scot-free. In others it may penalize an innocent person who might have been acquitted in court but was pressured into bargaining away his right to a trial. "The more experienced criminals," pointed out criminologist Donald Newman, "can manipulate legal processes to obtain light sentences and better official records while the less experienced, occasional offenders receive more harsh treatment."

The discretionary power used—and sometimes abused—by prosecutors and police is limited compared to that of the third branch of the criminal-justice system, the courts, which retain ultimate control of all parts of the system. They can order action to be taken by any of the other branches, or counter the effect of actions already taken. This supervisory role is only part of their general function of maintaining the peace by attempting to redress grievances committed against an individual or society by deciding whether or not a suspect is guilty and, if so, what penalty he should pay.

Courts often decided questions of guilt and innocence by resorting to the supernatural until fairly recently, even in the so-called more advanced societies.

Many peoples attributed killings to magic and looked to a dead man's body for clues to the identity of his murderer. The Kai tribes of New

Having located the suspect, McCain informs him of his legal rights and prepares, with her partner's aid, to handcuff him.

Holding the suspect securely so that he cannot escape, McCain politely but firmly escorts him to the station house.

continued

Guinea put betel in a dead man's mouth, thinking he would spit it out if his murderer came near. Certain tribes in Togo carried a dead man's body through the village with a stick pressed into his hand so he could use it to point out the magician who had done away with him. The first night after a death among the Narrenyerie of Australia, a relative would sleep with his head on the corpse, thus ensuring that he would dream of the guilty man. The English of the 16th Century knew that most deaths were natural, but in cases of actual murder they sometimes made the accused place his hand on the corpse. If the suspect was guilty, the wounds of the man he had killed would presumably bleed at his touch.

More commonly, evidence of guilt was expected not from the victim but from the suspect. In England until the early 19th Century, two suspects could settle the question of culpability in armed battle, on the theory that God would grant victory to the innocent. And trial by ordeal was an ancient and nearly universal practice. In parts of India, a suspect had to thrust his hand into a pot of earth to recover a buried ring —a test of innocence easy enough to pass if the pot had not also contained a live cobra. In ancient India and China, the test was to walk barefoot and blindfolded between red-hot plowshares. The early Japanese called on the accused to plunge his arm into boiling water; West Africans favored boiling oil.

At the station McKain watches vigilantly while the suspect is frisked. Not only weapons but items usable in a suicide attempt—his belt—are taken.

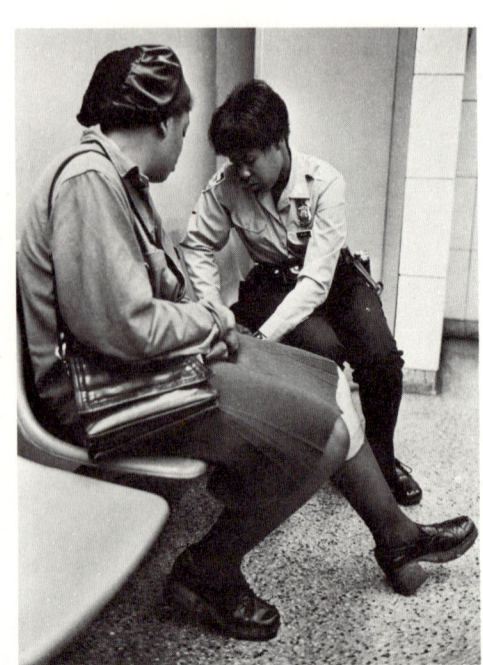

McKain (rear) takes down a statement from the bandaged victim describing the attack.

Many suspects, innocent and guilty alike, died in the course of such bizarre court procedures—few people doubted the fairness of trial by ordeal, and scores of people with nothing to hide demanded a chance to "prove" their innocence. As recently as the 19th Century, an estimated 40,000 to 50,000 inhabitants of Madagascar died in ordeals employing the poison tanghin, which paralyzes the heart muscle of one in five people who swallow it; a small tribe called the Uwet in Calabar became nearly extinct from this cause.

Safer—and much more effective at separating guilty from innocent—were bogus ordeals like one devised by a magistrate of ancient China. He told a suspected thief that he would have to submit to the bell-touching ordeal, and he explained that a particular temple bell would sound when touched by a guilty man but would remain silent at the touch of the innocent. Then the magistrate marched the suspect and all the other prisoners from the local jail to the temple. To underline the solemnity of the occasion, he offered a short prayer. Then he had a curtain hung in front of the bell, and he ordered all the prisoners to reach under it and touch the bell. After each prisoner had withdrawn his hand, the magistrate said the suspect's guilt was obvious, and the accused man immediately confessed.

The magistrate was not guessing. After the curtain was in place, he

The arresting officer types her report after the suspect has been fingerprinted, given a chance to call counsel and put in a holding pen.

Stepping aboard an armored van, McKain accompanies the suspect to court where he will be arraigned.

had secretly ordered the bell smeared with ink. All but one of the prisoners ended the ordeal with ink-stained fingers; only the suspect's hand was clean—he had not dared touch the bell for fear that it would actually sound forth his guilt.

The change from supernatural to rational standards of trial began long ago. As far back as 2500 B.C., the Egyptians weighed objective evidence in judging criminals, and starting about 1800 B.C., the Babylonians operated under the Code of Hammurabi, which prescribed an essentially modern court system that included professional judges, clerks and notaries.

Modern courts, recognizing the complexities of human behavior, do not take a simple black or white view of guilt or innocence. Not satisfied with finding out only whether a suspect did what he is accused of doing, they also want to know whether he intended to do it, and whether he did it voluntarily. If he did not, he is considered not truly guilty.

West German courts often find a defendant innocent by reason of intoxication. Most courts elsewhere, however, do not accept drunkenness as an excuse, and in the Soviet Union, evidence that a defendant was drunk counts heavily against him. In some countries in Europe and Latin America, mercy killing is accepted as legally permissible; it is not in Anglo-American courts, but it seldom brings a heavy sentence.

A verdict of innocent is also frequent if a defendant can show that external circumstances gave him little choice. One case often cited is that of a seaman named Holmes. In 1841, Holmes was a crewman aboard the American ship *William Brown*. When it sank in a storm, Holmes took to a lifeboat with 42 other passengers, far too many for the size of the boat. Heavy seas threatened to swamp it, and Holmes and some of the others threw 14 passengers overboard to lighten the load and save as many lives as possible.

When Holmes reached shore, he was charged with homicide. He argued that he should be found innocent because he had been acting under the doctrine of necessity. Under Anglo-American law, the doctrine holds that when a person is confronted with overwhelming natural forces, he may be compelled to choose between evils and do something that would be a crime in normal circumstances The court ruled that his behavior could be justified only if the sacrificed passengers had been chosen by lot or other impartial means. Since they had not, Holmes was found guilty. Experts, who still argue the case to this day, think if Holmes had been tried in a French or German court instead of an American one, he would have been freed.

A much commoner and more widely accepted defense in homicide cases is mental incapacity. In some courts, a defendant is judged insane and acquitted only if he did not know what he was doing or did not know it was against the law. This so-called M'Naghten Rule is criticized because most mentally ill people know what they are doing and can tell the difference between right and wrong, although they may not be able to stop themselves from breaking the law. To allow for such an "irresistible impulse," many courts now acquit defendants who were compelled by their mental state to commit crimes. A newer test of criminal responsibility is the Durham Rule, which was outlined by an American court in 1954: "An accused is not criminally responsible if his unlawful act was the product of mental disease or mental defect." The trouble with this rule is that unassailable proof of mental disease is difficult to establish.

The difficulty of assessing an accused person's responsibility is only part of the complexity of determining guilt or innocence—witnesses are never totally reliable, documentary evidence is often confusing, experts on "scientific" evidence disagree, and the laws themselves are ambiguous. In modern courts, the onerous task falls to judges or juries or, in some circumstances, to both together. A jury has become something of a rarity in Europe. Italy stopped using them in 1931, Spain in 1936 and France in 1941. Juries are still common in Austria, Belgium, Norway, parts of Switzerland, but only in very serious criminal cases in England. The United States Constitution guarantees the right to a jury trial in criminal cases although relatively few cases are disposed of in that way. In some instances, defendants prefer trial before a judge alone. In others, settlement is reached by dismissal or by a plea of guilt.

Skepticism about juries is often voiced by lawyers and social scientists as well as by some defendants. One of the most frequently heard criticisms is that juries cannot understand the complex issues that come up in courts of law. A study by Harry Kalven Jr. and Hans Zeisel seems to show the contrary. In 1954 and 1955 and again in 1958, the two law professors collected data on 3,576 criminal cases that had been tried by juries. Then they asked the judge in each case whether he agreed or disagreed with the jury's verdict of guilty or innocent and for what reasons. In 75 per cent of the cases, the judge said that if he had tried the case alone, he would have come to the same decision that had been reached by the jury.

A second argument against juries is that they allow personal biases to influence their deliberations. Several laboratory experiments seem to confirm that idea. For instance, a study by Harold Sigall and Nancy Ostrove of the University of Maryland suggested that a defendant's looks may exert an important effect on the jury's verdict. Sigall and Ostrove gave 40 students a detailed account of a fictitious burglary to read, along with a photograph of the supposed defendant. The descriptions of the crime did not vary, but the pictures did: half the students saw an unattractive girl, the other half, an attractive one. When the subjects were asked to sentence the criminal to anything from one to 15 years in prison, the unattractive burglar drew an average of 5.2 years, while the pretty one got away with a mere 2.8.

Joseph Sanders, a sociologist at the University of Michigan, acknowledges that such experiments "fuel the concern that juries employ legally irrelevant evidence in arriving at verdicts and that they disregard the judge's explanation of the law." But Sanders does not think the concern justified, and he believes he demonstrated as much in an experiment of his own conducted in 1975 and 1976.

Sanders enlisted 294 experienced former jurors to take part in his study and, dividing them into 49 "juries" of six members each, he had them deliberate in groups just as real juries do. He showed each of his juries one of eight versions of a videotaped simulated trial. The basic facts were the same in all eight versions: a defendant admitted removing some bricks from property that had burned down nine months earlier, and he claimed he thought the bricks had been abandoned. There were two variables. The first was the owner of the property. In half the versions of the trial, the bricks belonged to a private individual; in the other half, they belonged to the state of Michigan. Sanders' associate Diane Colasanto explained: "By varying . . . the 'size' of the victim, we examined whether the jury is influenced by irrelevant evidence. This is similar to the issue of defendant or victim attractiveness or character traits. We found no significant correlation between the identity of the victim and the final verdict."

The second variable was the judge's instruction to the jury. In half the trials, the judge told the jury to base its verdict on what lawyers call "general intent," in this case, simply to remove the bricks. In the rest of the trials, the judge said the verdict should be based on the concept of "specific intent," in this instance, to steal the bricks. In contrast to the first variable, the second affected the outcome of the mock deliberations. The juries told to decide general intent ruled "guilty," because the defendant had never denied that he had taken the bricks. However, most of the specific-intent juries either found the defendant not guilty or failed to reach any verdict at all, because although the defendant acknowledged taking the bricks, he thought that they had been abandoned

Under police guard, the announcer of German TV's "Case: XY... Unsolved" asks viewers to phone clues about crimes to detectives (rear).

Television programs to catch lawbreakers

Programs that invite the public to join in tracking down criminals are among the most popular of European television —and a real help to police. Every week 30 million armchair detectives in West Germany, Switzerland and Austria tune in on "Case: XY... Unsolved." After police review the particulars of several unsolved crimes, an announcer appeals to the audience to phone in leads to detectives, who sit behind a glass panel so that phones will not disturb the broadcast. To jog the memories of viewers who may have seen the suspect or witnessed the crime, the police display weapons, photographs of the scene or mug shots of suspects.

The program has helped solve an impressive 50 per cent of the cases aired. One productive tip came from an Austrian woman who had accepted a date with a man who politely offered to carry her packages. Before the rendezvous, she happened to see his picture on "Case: XY"; he was a hunted Swiss murderer. She contacted authorities and the man was arrested the next day.

Similar programs are aired in Spain, Hong Kong and a dozen British cities. The London version, "Police Five," has led Scotland Yard to an average of 100 arrests a year during the 15 years of the program's existence. But authorities believe the shows' biggest contribution is in engendering cooperation between people and police in fighting crime.

and did not admit any specific intent to steal. "This shows that juries do, in fact, pay close attention to the judge's instructions and that they take their responsibility very seriously." One reason the jury system works, Sanders added, is that "juries reach their decisions together, after much thoughtful sharing of opinions. We believe that juries usually weigh and interpret evidence in the light of the specific instructions the judge gives them."

Instructing members of the jury in the law as it applies to the case they are deciding is only one function of a modern judge. Overall, his job is to supervise the questioning of witnesses and the presentation of evidence by both prosecution and defense. When disputes arise, he acts as a neutral arbiter. Of course, when there is no jury, it is up to the judge himself to elicit testimony, decide which version of events is most credible and pronounce a verdict. Whether there is a jury or not, it is the judge in most courts who determines the penalty, if any, that a convicted criminal must pay.

"When I was on the bench, I believed in creative sentencing," says Charles Smith, who became Associate Dean of the University of Washington law school after eight years as a judge. One defendant who came before him was an elderly man charged with procurement. "He was a lonely old man," Smith remembers, "who probably did what he did in part to surround himself with people. He could have been given a maximum of 20 years, but I didn't see any point in just putting him away for what would probably have been the rest of his life."

The defendant had been involved in organized crime off and on most of his life and had amassed a good deal of money. But Smith thought even a heavy fine would be pointless. "Since he had spent most of his life degrading women, I ordered him to establish a trust fund for the education of women who had been prostitutes and wanted a new way of life. I had no expectations that this was going to change lives magically, but at least I thought it would be beneficial." One of the beneficiaries was a prostitute who heard of the trust fund, finished high school, began studying for a university degree and went to work as a research assistant to an anthropologist.

It is seldom as easy to make the punishment fit the crime as it was for Judge Smith. Another judge interviewed by the American psychiatrist Willard Gaylin described the dilemma he had faced in sentencing a man who had shot his son: "The father killed the boy, and he should have been sent to prison. And yet, the *feeling* was that the father loved the boy, and was trying to do the best thing for the boy, but was driven to this incident which caused the unfortunate accident when he fired a warning shot and the kid moved into the line of fire.... I gave him probation. He was a physician, an outstanding physician, and I received hundreds of letters on his behalf. But some said I was still too generous. Others said ... the father was hurt enough. So you're damned if you do and damned if you don't."

Such great discretionary power leads to staggering disparities in sentencing, generally in favor of the rich and powerful at the expense of the poor and weak. To Gaylin, these disparities are so enormous that they eat away at "the basic structural prop of equity that supports our sense of justice."

In 1975, American investigators sent 50 judges basic facts about 20 actual cases and asked them what penalty they would impose in each. In one case the defendant had been found guilty of possessing drugs with intent to distribute them; one judge put him on probation, while another sentenced him to five years in prison. In another case, the defendant was a middle-aged union official convicted of extortion; one judge said he should serve three years, while a second gave him 20 years plus a fine of $65,000.

A few years ago, the solution to such problems was thought to be indeterminate sentencing, in which an offender is sent to prison without specifying how long he must stay. He is released only when a parole board or some other agency decides he has been rehabilitated. In the United States, this method of sentencing is widely used, and as widely criticized. One study called it "one of the more exquisite forms of torture" because it gives parole boards great power and leaves prisoners at the mercy of officials who may impose arbitrary standards of conduct and outlook as the price for freedom.

Two other schemes, calling for either "flat time" or "presumptive" sentencing, have been urged. Under the first, legislatures would set precisely the same sentences for equivalent crimes. Petty theft might mean a two-year prison term, while armed robbery might be pegged at eight years. These sentences would be mandatory and could be shortened only under rigid rules. Presumptive sentencing also would begin with a specified penalty for each type and degree of crime. But for every mitigating or aggravating circumstance, the judge would shorten or lengthen the sentence by a specified percentage. If a defendant had previously been convicted of armed robbery, for example, his presumptive sentence might be increased by 25 per cent, to two and a half years.

Such proposals aim to put into practice the old idea that the punishment ought to fit the crime. To provide a rational, fair basis for this

Chapter 5

Inmates of a South Carolina prison camp overflow cells and sleep on mattresses in a corridor. Severe overcrowding in many American prison facilities followed a sharp rise in the prison population in the mid-1970s—variously attributed to economic conditions, an increase in the number of young adults and a greater emphasis on punishment—adding to court-ordered punishment another kind of punishment that was never intended.

kind of system, Marvin Wolfgang and his associates at the University of Pennsylvania have attempted to establish a scale of crime—least offensive to most offensive—with a corresponding scale of penalties. They interviewed some 75,000 Americans, asking them to rate 141 criminal actions, from disorderly conduct and bicycle theft to rape and murder, on a point system—1 for the action considered least serious to 11 for the most serious. The same people were also asked to rate punishments, from a $15 fine to life imprisonment. Crimes were then paired with penalties that had been given the same average point score.

The concern about the fairness of sentencing is one indication of contemporary ambivalence about the value of punishment. In an earlier age, such doubts were rare. Yet punishment was much harsher than it is today. In some societies, the penalty for sorcery or sacrilege was the obliteration of entire villages: inhabitants, livestock, buildings and trees. The wrongdoers were thought to have contaminated everyone and everything around them by crimes that offended the gods, and unless authorities took drastic protective measures, people reasoned, the gods might retaliate against a whole nation.

Until well into the 18th Century, corporal punishment was common practice. Criminals were beaten with knouts, confined in sweatboxes, deprived of food and water, branded with hot irons or forced to submit to amputation of their hands. Banishment to remote labor colonies was frequent. Death by stoning, drowning and burning was decreed even for minor offenses.

Gradually, people began to believe that a person who breaks the law retains his humanity just the same, and physical punishment came to be seen as barbaric. By 1976, the death penalty had been eliminated in Austria, Italy, Portugal, Scandinavia, Switzerland, West Germany and a few other countries; where it survived, it was imposed chiefly for murder or treason. In the 20th Century, the most important remaining penal sanctions were imprisonment or some form of probation or parole that permitted an offender to live in the community under supervision.

When a society punishes an offender, it has one or more goals in mind: to avenge the community; to rehabilitate, or "cure," the wrongdoer so he will never want to break the law again; to deter him from committing more crimes by making the price he has to pay too high, and to deter others who witness his punishment; or to protect society by isolating the criminal.

At one time, most people believed it was right to exact retribution through punishment. In 1883, the English jurist Sir James Stephen maintained that "criminals should be hated" and that "the punishments inflicted upon them should be so contrived as to give expression to that hatred." Yet there have always been those to whom vengeance was anathema. As early as 2100 B.C. King Ur-Nammu of Sumeria forbade his subjects to inflict pain or other vengeful penalties on criminals.

Although vengeance as a motive for punishing criminals has gone underground, only the naïve imagine that it has disappeared. Such "respectable" motives for punishment as rehabilitation, deterrence and protection are often just cloaks for vengeance, in the opinion of many.

The idea of punishing criminals not to get back at them but to rehabilitate them came into its own in the 18th Century. At first the goal was reformation through penitence; hence the word penitentiary. The theory was that criminals would mend their ways if they served out their sentences in solitary confinement with nothing to do but read the Bible and ponder their evil ways. This experiment turned out to be as fruitless as later attempts to reform criminals through treatment, either by psychological therapies or in work and study programs. More than two thirds of offenders commit new crimes after their release from confinement. Sociologist Robert Martinson, having studied hundreds of programs over a period of two decades, concluded, "The prison which makes every effort at rehabilitation succeeds no better than the prison which leaves its inmates to rot." Historian David Rothman called rehabilitation "the noble lie."

Some people think it need not be so, that given the will, and the money, rehabilitation can become a reality instead of a lie. One complaint leveled at the average prison is that it exiles the criminal from living and that this is poor preparation for going straight after release. "It's hard to train an aviator in a submarine," criminologist Hans Mattick observed. A second obstacle to rehabilitation, according to reformers, is the dehumanizing harshness of prison existence. "Men are not improved by injuries," George Bernard Shaw wrote in his essay *The Crime of Imprisonment.*

Sweden's correctional system goes a long way toward meeting such objections. When an American visitor suggested to the warden of a maximum security Swedish prison that he could reduce the number of escapes by topping the prison wall with barbed wire, the warden's response typified his country's concern for its criminals. "We couldn't do that," he said in shocked tones. "The prisoners might hurt themselves." Swedish offenders are considered citizens who deserve respect and a fairly high standard of living *(pages 165-167).* "I don't believe in punishment or in prisons," said Torsten Eriksson, a top prison official in Sweden. "It is necessary to incarcerate certain people to protect so-

continued on page 168

In the love room of a Swedish prison, a convict kisses his wife and cuddles his child during one of their frequent visits. Private quarters for intimate personal meetings are only one among the special facilities provided to preserve normal relationships that, in the Swedish view, aid the criminal's return to society.

Soft stretch in a Swedish prison

The Swedes hold an unusual attitude toward crime, believing that the state has an obligation to the primary victim —the criminal. This view, attuned to the peculiar mixture of authoritarianism and compassion distinguishing the country's social system, is put into practice in prisons, which look less like jails than vacation resorts—as a few are *(overleaf)*. Some have walls but few other protective aspects. Many of the prisoners—called clients—live in private rooms with television sets, and all share pantries, swimming pools, miniature golf courses and "love rooms," where they may entertain female visitors. Since Swedish prisoners are sent to prisons near their homes whenever possible, these visits are frequent.

If the walled prisons are unusual, the open prisons scarcely warrant the name. In them, inmates come and go at will; they have keys to their own rooms and entertain visitors in them.

Prison sentences are short—usually less than four months—and even during these brief stays prisoners with good behavior are entitled to furloughs away from prison. No evidence from crime rates or rehabilitation statistics indicates that Sweden's coddling works better than the strict measures common elsewhere. But neither is there evidence that it works worse.

165

Practicing newly learned skills, an inmate concentrates on welding a metal basket. Prisoners work, learning a trade if necessary, so that they will be self-supporting. They are paid the going rate for the work they perform.

A prisoner and a guard enjoy a game of pool in one of their prison's recreation rooms, where paperback books are also available. Such fraternization is encouraged, and rapport between inmates and highly trained prison staff is high.

Prisoners and their families stroll through a holiday village established for them. Like all Swedes, convicts are entitled to a month-long vacation.

ciety. But once we have incarcerated them, we must work against the prison, that is, protect the prisoners from it."

In one Swedish experiment, the Family Prison, a convict lives at home with his wife and takes a job in the community. Among the first assigned to the program was Gunnar, a 30-year-old murderer. Except for 12 hours of freedom on weekends, Gunnar had to spend his nonworking hours at home, and he was expected to call or see prison officials once every week. Otherwise his life was like that of any ordinary Swede. He got up at six every morning to reach his road construction job 10 miles from his home. Then he cycled back for dinner, prepared by his wife. Afterward the two of them relaxed by watching television or entertaining their friends.

Few would argue that this rehabilitation-oriented Family Prison could achieve the third major aim of punishment, deterrence, for a penalty that is meant to discourage crime has to be distinctly unpleasant. Plato was one of the first advocates of penalties to achieve deterrence rather than revenge. No one, he said, should be punished "because he did wrong, for that which is done can never be undone, but in order that in future times he, and those who see him corrected, may abate much of their evil-doing."

Whether or not punishment actually abates criminal behavior is controversial. Many authorities think it does not. They point out that in the 18th Century, when pickpocketing was a capital crime, practitioners of that trade were invariably present at public executions, not looking on in chastened horror but diligently practicing their skills on careless men and women enthralled by the spectacle of death. Also frequently cited is a 1959 study by sociologist Thorsten Sellin, which found that murder occurred just about as often in states that imposed the death penalty as in those that did not. He also found no important change in homicide rates after a state had either abolished or restored capital punishment.

A great many criminologists are unconvinced by such arguments. They maintain that punishment can be made to deter, not by increasing its severity but by increasing its certainty. In 1972 George Antunes of Rice University and A. Lee Hunt of the University of Houston analyzed the studies of other researchers and concluded that, when a high proportion of people charged with a particular crime were imprisoned, incidence of that crime tended to be low. Conversely, where the rate of imprisonment was low, the crime occurred more often.

Antunes and Hunt found that long prison terms had no greater deterrent value than short ones. In fact, psychiatrist Edward Stainbrook became convinced that long sentences may actually promote crime. "After a certain point, time in prison no longer deters, but begins increasing hostility," Stainbrook said. "Then you just worsen the problem you're trying to cure."

Norwegian professor of law Johannes Andenaes cited a persuasive example of punishment as a deterrent. In the United States, drunken driving is common; in Norway, driving after even moderate drinking is rare. Andenaes attributed the difference to the fact that Norwegian courts nearly always impose a prison sentence for driving under the influence of alcohol, while American courts rarely do. In Norway the possibility of going to jail is "a living reality to every driver," Andenaes wrote, and "for most people the risk seems too great."

The value of punishment inflicted for purposes of vengeance, rehabilitation or deterrence is often questioned, but no one denies that imprisonment for the purpose of protecting law-abiding citizens inevitably works—so long as the offender remains incarcerated. As argument over the effectiveness of deterrence continues and disillusionment with rehabilitation grows, many authorities maintain that society might get the best practical results by increasing its reliance on imprisonment for protection.

Marvin Wolfgang suggested that society should concentrate on identifying and convicting the very few criminals—perhaps 6 per cent—who have committed three or more offenses; this small minority of troublemakers is responsible for two thirds of all violent crimes in the United States. Such hard-core repeaters, Wolfgang recommended, should be "incapacitated," that is, imprisoned for irreducible terms so that they could not harm society for the duration of their sentences. If this group of offenders were jailed for three years, crime researchers Shlomo and Reuel Shinnar calculated, the rate of serious crime should drop to a third of what it is today.

Perhaps more surprising is the fact that a growing number of criminologists have come to advocate punishment not for rehabilitation, deterrence, or even protection but for its own sake. "Certain things are simply wrong and ought to be punished," maintained historian David Rothman and psychoanalyst Willard Gaylin. "When we honestly face the fact that our purpose is retributive, we may, with a re-found compassion and a renewed humanity, limit the degree of retribution we will exact." With such reexaminations of the ways society attempts to deal with criminal behavior, scholars of many disciplines seek to bring closer the age-old dream of mankind: a life in which every person feels secure from harm to his person or his property.

Bibliography

Alexander, Franz, and William Healy, *Roots of Crime*. Patterson Smith Publishing Corp., 1935.
Benjamin, Harry, and R. E. L. Masters, *Prostitution and Morality*. The Julian Press, Inc., 1964.
Blumberg, Abraham S., ed., *Current Perspectives on Criminal Behavior*. Alfred A. Knopf, 1974.
Bromberg, Walter:
 Crime and the Mind. The Macmillan Company, 1965.
 The Mold of Murder. Greenwood Press, 1961.
Cameron, Mary Owen, *The Booster and the Snitch*. The Free Press, 1964.
Cressey, Donald R.:
 Other People's Money. The Free Press, 1953.
 Theft of the Nation. Harper & Row, Publishers, 1969.
Davidson, David, *The Story of the Century*. American Heritage Press, 1976.
Durham, Michael, "For the Swedes a Prison Sentence Can Be Fun," *Smithsonian*, September 1973.
Gaylin, Willard, *Partial Justice*. Alfred A. Knopf, 1974.
Geis, Gilbert, ed., *The White-Collar Criminal*. Atherton Press, 1968.
Glueck, Sheldon, ed., *The Problem of Delinquency*. Houghton Mifflin Co., 1959.
Goldstein, Abraham S., *The Insanity Defense*. Yale University Press, 1967.
Goodman, Walter, *All Honorable Men*. Little, Brown and Company, 1963.
Gosling, John, and Dennis Craig, *The Great Train Robbery*. The Bobbs-Merrill Company, Inc., 1965.
Halleck, Seymour L., *Psychiatry and the Dilemmas of Crime*. University of California Press, 1971.
Hamilton, Charles, ed., *Men of the Underworld*. The Macmillan Company, 1952.
Ianni, Francis A. J., and Elizabeth Reuss-Ianni, *A Family Business*. Russell Sage Foundation, 1972.
Jackson, Richard, *Occupied with Crime*. Doubleday & Company, Inc., 1967.
Jaspan, Norman, *The Thief in the White Collar*. J. B. Lippincott Co., 1960.
Josephson, Matthew, *The Robber Barons*. Harcourt, Brace and Company, 1934.
Kalven, Harry, Jr., and Hans Zeisel, *The American Jury*. Little, Brown and Company, 1966.
Kobler, John:
 Ardent Spirits. G. P. Putnam's Sons, 1973.
 Capone. G. P. Putnam's Sons, 1971.
Lindner, Robert M., *Rebel without a Cause*. Grune and Stratton, Publishers, 1944.
Mack, John A., and Hans-Jürgen Kerner, *The Crime Industry*. Saxon House, 1975.
Mann, Martin, *Peacetime Uses of Atomic Energy*. Thomas Y. Crowell Company, 1975.
Maurer, David W., *Whiz Mob*. College & University Press, 1964.
Menninger, Karl:
 The Crime of Punishment. The Viking Press, 1966.
 Man against Himself. Harcourt, Brace and Company, 1938.
 The Vital Balance. The Viking Press, 1963.
Montet, Pierre, *Everyday Life in Egypt*. Edward Arnold Ltd., 1962.
Muller, Herbert Joseph, *The Spirit of Tragedy*. Alfred A. Knopf, 1956.
Myers, Gustavus, *History of the Great American Fortunes*, 3 vols. Charles H. Kerr & Company, 1908-1910.
Nader, Ralph, and Mark J. Green, eds., *Corporate Power in America*. Grossman Publishers, 1973.
Nader, Ralph, Mark Green and Joel Seligman, *Taming the Giant Corporation*. W. W. Norton & Company, Inc., 1976.
O'Connor, Richard, *Gould's Millions*. Doubleday & Company, Inc., 1962.
The President's Commission on Law Enforcement and Administration of Justice, *Task Force Report: Crime and Its Impact—an Assessment*. U.S. Government Printing Office, 1967.
 The Challenge of Crime in a Free Society. U.S. Government Printing Office, 1967.
Radzinowicz, Leon, and Marvin E. Wolfgang, eds., *Crime and Justice*, Vol. II, *The Criminal in the Arms of the Law*. Basic Books, Inc., 1971.
Reik, Theodor, *The Compulsion to Confess*. Grove Press, Inc., 1961.
Schur, Edwin M., *Our Criminal Society*. Prentice-Hall, Inc., 1969.
Scott, Harald, ed., *Crime and Criminals*. Hawthorn Books Inc., 1961.
Sellin, Thorsten, *The Death Penalty*. The American Law Institute, 1959.
Shaw, George Bernard, *The Crime of Imprisonment*. The Citadel Press, 1961.
Smith, J. M. Powis, *The Origin and History of Hebrew Law*. The University of Chicago Press, 1960.
Tracy, John Evarts, *Nine Famous Trials*. Vantage Press, 1960.
Von Hirsch, Andrew, *Doing Justice*. Hill and Wang, 1976.
Waller, George, *Kidnap: The Story of the Lindbergh Case*. The Dial Press, 1961.
Warshow, Robert, *The Immediate Experience*. Doubleday & Co., Inc., 1962.
Willwerth, James, *Jones*. M. Evans and Company, Inc., 1974.
Wilson, James Q., *Thinking about Crime*. Basic Books, Inc., 1975.
Wolfgang, Marvin E., Leonard Savitz and Norman Johnston, eds., *The Sociology of Crime and Delinquency*. John Wiley & Sons, Inc., 1970.

Acknowledgments

Portions of this book were written by Mike Roberts. The index was prepared by Gale Partoyan. The editors also wish to thank the following persons and institutions for their assistance in the preparation of this book: Dr. John Baldwin, Institute of Judicial Administration, University of Birmingham, Birmingham, England; Lieutenant Frank Bolz, New York City Police Department, New York; Professor R. L. Carter, Nottingham University, Nottingham, England; Claude Charmes, Editor, *Promovere* magazine, Paris; Professor Francesco Di Girolamo, Director, Institute of Observation, Rebibbia Prison, Rome; Professor Benigno di

Tullio, President, International Society of Criminology, Rome; Jean Druesne, Police Superintendent, Ministère de l'Intérieur, Paris; William K. Everson, New York University, New York; Federal Bureau of Statistics, Wiesbaden, Germany; Professor Franco Ferracuti, Department of Clinical Criminology, University of Rome, Rome; Dr. Maria Pia Frangeamore, Assistant Director, Institute of Observation, Rebibbia Prison, Rome; Mary Gluckman, Stockport, Cheshire, England; Pierre Grelley, Centre de Formation et de Recherche de l'Éducation Surveillée, Vaucresson, France; Nicholas Hinton, National Association for the Care and Resettlement of Offenders, London; Commandant Yves Majorel, Ministère de l'Intérieur, Paris; Professor F. H. McClintock, Edinburgh University, Edinburgh; Professor Virginia Morris, John Jay College of Criminal Justice, New York, New York; The Police Academy of the Tokyo Metropolitan Police Board, Tokyo; Pierrette Poncela, Institute de Criminologie de Paris II, Paris; Philippe Robert, Service d'Études, Pénales et Criminologiques, Paris; Paul Roche, Press Attaché, Préfecture de Police, Paris; Dr. Yves Roumajon, Paris; Dr. Joseph Sanders, University of Michigan, Ann Arbor, Michigan; William Studer, Press Attaché, Ministère de l'Intérieur, Paris; Ian Taylor, Sheffield University, Sheffield, England; Professor Sergio Tovo, Director, Museum of Criminal Anthropology, University of Turin, Turin, Italy; Jacques Vérin, Deputy Public Prosecutor, Ministry of Justice, Paris.

Picture Credits

The sources for illustrations in this book are shown below. Credits for illustrations from left to right are separated by semicolons, from top to bottom by dashes.

Cover—Duane Michals. 6—The Kansas State Historical Society, Topeka. 10, 11—Rizzoli Press from Photoreporters. 12, 13—John Loengard from TIME-LIFE Picture Agency; Bill Eppridge from TIME-LIFE Picture Agency; Fred Ritchin—Bill Eppridge from TIME-LIFE Picture Agency except center, Steven Mazawa from TIME-LIFE Picture Agency. 16, 17—Jenaro Olivares for *Novedades*. 18—Copyright © by Brassaï. 20, 21—Homer Sykes/VIVA from Woodfin Camp and Associates. 24, 25—Gérard Rancinan from Sygma. 28, 29—New York *Daily News*. 30, 31—Wide World except background, © 1932 by The New York Times Company, reprinted by permission. 32—Wide World (2)—*The Morning Tribune*, New Orleans. 33—*The New York Times*. 34, 35—United Press International; Wide World—New York *Daily News*, photographed by Frank Lerner courtesy Newspaper Annex, The New York Public Library, Astor, Lenox and Tilden Foundations; *The Los Angeles Times*. 36, 37—United Press International—*The New York Times*/background, *The Washington Post* courtesy Library of Congress. 38, 39—Wide World—New York *Daily News*; *Chicago Daily Times*. 40—Jacob A. Riis Collection, Museum of the City of New York. 44, 45—Top row, K. Chester from TIME-LIFE Picture Agency (3); United Press International (2); K. Chester from TIME-LIFE Picture Agency—center row, Wide World; United Press International; Wide World; K. Chester from TIME-LIFE Picture Agency (3)—bottom row, United Press International; K. Chester from TIME-LIFE Picture Agency; Eric Schaal from TIME-LIFE Picture Agency; United Press International (2). 51—The March of Time. 52—Italy's News Photos. 56, 57—Leonard Freed from Magnum. 60, 61—Theatre Collection, The New York Public Library at Lincoln Center, Astor, Lenox and Tilden Foundations. 62, 63—John Hugelmeyer from TIME-LIFE Picture Agency; McKague courtesy Stratford Festival, Canada. 64—Henry W. and Albert A. Berg Collection, The New York Public Library, Astor, Lenox and Tilden Foundations. 65—Culver Pictures. 66, 67—Film Stills Archive, Museum of Modern Art; from a wood engraving made by Fritz Eichenberg for an edition of *Crime and Punishment* issued by The Heritage Club, copyright © 1938, 1966, reproduced by arrangement with The Heritage Press, Inc., Westport, Connecticut, courtesy Rare Book Division, The New York Public Library, Astor, Lenox and Tilden Foundations. 68—Prints Division, The New York Public Library, Astor, Lenox and Tilden Foundations. 69—Culver Pictures. 70—Gilles Peress from Magnum. 74—Philippe Ledru from Sygma. 77—Topix. 81—United Press International. 82, 83—TIME-LIFE Picture Agency—Yale Joel from TIME-LIFE Picture Agency; Ivo Meldolesi for *The New York Times*; Topix. 86—Bruno A. Sulzer from TIME-LIFE Picture Agency. 87—Provided by Ankara Narcotic Police Archives. 88, 89—George Silk from TIME-LIFE Picture Agency. 91—Camera Press. 94, 95—Leonard Freed from Magnum. 98, 99—United Press International—Chicago Historical Society; *Chicago Tribune*; United Press International—Chicago Historical Society. 100, 101—*Chicago Tribune* except upper left, United Press International. 102, 103—Margaret Bourke-White for FORTUNE except upper right, *Chicago Tribune*. 104, 105—TIME-LIFE Picture Agency. 106, 107—*Chicago Tribune*; Chicago Historical Society. 108, 109—*Chicago Tribune*; Brown Brothers—United Press International. 110, 111—Chicago Historical Society. 112—ANSA. 116, 117—The Bettmann Archive except center, courtesy The Bancroft Library. 119—Burk Uzzle from Magnum. Overlapping chart based on statistics provided by the Chamber of Commerce of the U.S., Washington, D.C. 122, Alain Déjean from Sygma. 125—United Press International. 126, 127—Edwin Levick from TIME-LIFE Picture Agency—Inset, United Press International; Dick Sarvo for the *New York Mirror*. 130, 131—*Yomiuri Shimbun*, Tokyo. 133—Don Carl Steffen from TIME-LIFE Picture Agency. 136—Bill Stanton from Magnum. 140—United Press International. 143 to 146—Rick Smolan/Contact. 149—Wide World. 152 to 155—Sepp Seitz from Magnum. 159—Krämer, *Stern*. 162—South Carolina Department of Corrections. 165, 166, 167—John Dominis from TIME-LIFE Picture Agency.

Index

Numerals in italics indicate a photograph or drawing of the subject mentioned.

A
Abortion laws, 22
Adams, Charles and Henry, quoted, 117
Adams, John, 115
African tribes, 58
Alcatraz prison, 46
Alcmaeonid family (ancient Greece), 113, 118
Alcohol laws, 23
Alexander, Franz, 50
Algeria, 19
Allchin, W. H., quoted, 49
Allport, Gordon, 147
Amenson, Sigrid, 50
American Psychological Association, 59
Amnesty International, 148
Anastasia, Albert, *88-89*
Andenaes, Johannes, 169
Antunes, George, 168
Arab terrorists, 141, 142
Art, crime portrayed in, *60-69*
Art forgeries, 17, 81, *82*
Art thefts (Italy), *10-11*
Asinara island, L (penal colony), *94-95*
Australia, Narrenyerie people of, 154
Austria, 86; criminal-justice system, 157, 163
Automobile theft, 96; Europe, 86-87

B
B as in Banshee (Treat), 46
Bacon, Sir Francis, 114
Bad-seed theories, 43-48
Baltimore, Maryland, *140*
Bandura, Albert, 59
Banghart, Basil "The Owl," *44-46*
Bank robberies, 6, 9, *74*, 81, *82*
Bankruptcies, fraud and, *118-119*
Banfield, Edward, quoted, 58
Banton, Michael, quoted, 148-149
Bard, Morton, 140
Barrow, Clyde, 81
Basque terrorists (Spain), *24-25*
Behan, Neil, 141
Belgium, 86; juries, 157; Lockheed crisis, 115
Bell, Daniel, quoted, 19
Belmondo, Jean-Paul, 15
Benjamin, Harry, quoted, 80
Benny, Jack, 36
Bergbreiter, Jacob, 97
Berkowitz, Bernard, 140
Berns, Charlie, quoted, 22
Bert, Pierre, *118-120*
Biddle, Nicholas, 114
Biological theories, 43-49, *44-45*
Blacks, racial discrimination and, 57, 58
Blochman, Lawrence G., *44-46*
Blood on Nassau's Moon (McCully), 46
"Body type" classifications, 46-47
Bohannan, Paul, 58
Bolz, Frank, *142*; quoted, 141
Bombay Mail (Blochman), 46
Bonnie and Clyde (film), 15
Boosters (professional shoplifters), 76-78
Bootlegging, 87-90, 98, *100-101*. See also Capone, Al
Bormann, Martin, 15
Boston, Massachusetts, 14
"Bovver birds" (London), 9, 26
Brain damage theory, 48-49
Brezhnev, Leonid, 134
Bribery. See Corruption

C
Camus, Albert, 61; *The Stranger*, 69
Capone, Al, 46, 84, *98-111*
Capone, Albert (Sonny), *109*
Capone, Frank, *106-107*
Capone (Kobler), 100
"Case: XY . . . Unsolved" (German TV program), *159*
Castellamarese war (1930-1931), 90
Caveat emptor v. *caveat vendor*, 129
Chaplin, Charles, 61; *Monsieur Verdoux*, 64, 65
Chicago, Illinois, 14, 97; Capone and, 100, *104-105*, 109; Touhy gang, 46
Child abuse, *20-21*, 41, 53, *56-57*
China (ancient), 154, 155-156
Chinese ghettos, 57
Chkekheidze, T., 134
Choisy, Maryse, quoted, 80
Christie, Agatha, 14
Chromosome studies, 47-48
Cline, Alfred, *44-46*
Cloward, Richard, quoted, 54-55
Colasanto, Diane, quoted, 158
Coleridge, Samuel Taylor, *The Rime of the Ancient Mariner*, *68*, 69
Colombia, 55
Communist countries, white-collar crime in, 134-135. See also Soviet Union
Condon, Dr. John F., *32-33*
Confessions, 147-148
Confidence men, 76, 79-80
Corruption, 97, 115, 129
"Cosa Nostra, La," 87, 93. See also Organized crime
Costs, of white-collar crime, *118-119*
Counterfeiting, 139
Courts, 153-169; judges and, *160-161*; juries and, *157-160*; and punishment (sentencing), 161-169
Cox, Herbert, 71-72
Creative analyses of crime, *60-69*
Credit cards, Mafia and, 96
Cressey, Donald, 121-123, 128; quoted, 87, 90, 93
Crime and Punishment (Dostoevsky), 67
Crime commissions (United States), 54; President's Crime Commission, 73, 87
Crime of Imprisonment, The (Shaw), 164
Crime Quiz (radio show), 46
Crime statistics, 8-11
Crime-as-alternative hypothesis, 49
Crimes "against the person," 17. See also Murder
Criminal, The (Ellis), 46
Criminal Man, The (Lombroso), 43-46
Criminologists: artists compared to, 61; biological theories of, 43-49; psychological theories of, 49-53; sociological theories of, 53-59
Crocker, Charles, *116-117*
Cruse, Lionel and Ivan, 118, *122*
Curtis, John Hughes, *30*

D
D as in Dead (Treat), 46
Dacoits (India), *26-27*
Dannay, Frederic, 46
Death Rides a Tandem (McCully), 46
Death sentence, *38-39*, 41, 51, 163
Decoy technique of police, *149*
Defenses, 156-157
Delinquent (criminal) subcultures, 55
Detective stories, 14, 61
Detroit, Michigan, 9
Dickens, Charles, *Oliver Twist*, 64
Disguise, art of, 81
Distilled Liquors Corporation, 125
Doctrine of necessity, 156
Dostoevsky, Feodor, *Crime and Punishment*, 67
Drew, Daniel, 129
Drugs: addicts, 10, 17; laws, 23; smuggling, 87, 92, 96
Durham Rule, 157

E
Eastman, Monk, quoted, 8
Ectomorphs, 47
Edmonds, John, quoted, 141
Egyptians (ancient), 156
Eichenberg, Fritz, 67
"Electrical conspiracy" (1961), 124-128, 129
Ellis, Havelock, 43-46; *The Criminal*, 46
Embezzling, *118-119*, 121-123, 128
Endomorphs, 47
England, 9, 10; Great Train Robbery (1963), 15, 77; organized crime, 85-86; white-collar

crime, 128, 129; juries, 157; police, 148-150. See also London; Scotland Yard
Eriksson, Torsten, quoted, 164-168
European Economic Community, 86
Express, L' (French newspaper), 9
Extortion, 83, 85-86, 96
Eye-witness testimony, 142-147

F
Family quarrels, police and, 139-141
Fear of crime, 14; signs of, *12-13*
Fear over the City (film), 15
Fences, 96
Ferber, Edna, quoted, 36
Field, Cyrus, *117*
Films, crime portrayed in, 14-15
Fiorenza, John, *44-46*
Florida: Capone and, *108-109*; organized crime in, 90
Fontanne, Lynn, 36
Forgeries (art), 81, *82*
Fortescue, Sir John, 57
Fortune Society, 53
France, 9, 11-14, 58; criminal-justice system in, 148, 151, 157; organized crime in, 85; prostitution in, *18*; white-collar crime in, 114, 118-120, *122*. See also Paris
Frankfurt, Germany, 10
Fraud(s): bankruptcies and, *118-119*; Ipecac, 120-121, 135; long-term, 85; tax, 11, 114; wine, 118-120, *122*. See also Confidence men
Freud, Sigmund, 52; quoted, 50-51, 138
Funerals (gangland), *106-107*
Furtseva, Yekaterina A., 134

G
Gambling (illegal), 92-93; and embezzling, 122
Gangland executions, *88-89*, *106-107*
Gangs: Glasgow, 42; New York City, 7, 73. See also Organized crime
Gaylin, Willard, 160; quoted, 121, 135, 161, 169
Geis, Gilbert, quoted, 23, 57, 124
Genetics, 47-48
Genna, Bloody Angelo, *107*
Genna, Jim, *98-99*
Genoa, Italy, *10-11*
Germany, see West Germany
Ghettos, ethnic, 57
Gibbens, Trevor, quoted, 26
Giuliano, Salvatore, *82-83*
Glasgow, Scotland, 42
Glueck, Eleanor and Sheldon, 47
Godfather, The (film), 15
Goring, Charles, quoted, 46
Gould, Jay, *117*
Gould, Leroy, quoted, 73, 84
Great Train Robbery (England, 1963), 15, 75-76, *77*

Greece (ancient), 17, 51; playwrights, *62-63*; white-collar crime in, 113, 118
"Grifters," 73, 76-80
Guilt, 50-51
Guns, police and, 148-150

H
Hacker, Frederick, 59
Halleck, Seymour, quoted, 49, 59
Halliday, Brett, *44-46*
Hammurabi Code, 138, 156
Hanging, 41, 51. See also Death sentence
Harlem Railroad, 129
Hartnett, Gabby, *109*
Hartung, Frank, quoted, 54
Hauptmann, Bruno Richard, 29, *34-39*
Healy, William, 50
Heard, Alexander, 97
"Heavies," 73-76, 79
Herostratus, 51
Hijacking cases, 139
Highway robbery, 7
Hoffman, Margaret, *65*
Hong Kong, 85
Hormone theory, 48
Hory, Elmyr de, 81, *82*
Hostages, police and, 141-142
How to Be a Detective (book), 71
Hubbard, David, quoted, 25
Hugon, Daniel, 47-48
Hunt, A. Lee, 168
Hunt, E. Howard, 118
Hustling, defined, 73

I
Ianni, Francis, quoted, 90-92, 93
Iceberg Slim (pimp), quoted, 84
Illinois, organized crime in, 90. See also Chicago, Illinois
India, 154; Dacoits, 26-27
Infanticide, 17
Interpol (International Criminal Police Organization), 138-139
Ipecac fraud, 120-121, 135
Irwin, Robert, quoted, 51
Ishii, Ichiro, 85
Israelis, terrorists and, 141, 142
Italian-Americans, 26
Italy, *10-11*, 14, *52*, 58, 86; abortion, 22; criminal-justice system, 148, 157, 163; drug laws, 23; white-collar crime in, *112*, 114, 118, 120. See also Sicily
Izvestia (Soviet newspaper), 8

J
Jack the Ripper, *51*
Jackson, Andrew, 114
Jackson, Sir Richard, quoted, 85
Japan, 11; abortion, 22; ancient, 154; drug laws, 23; Lockheed crisis, 115, *130-131*, 132-

134; organized crime in, 27, 85; police, *143-146*, 148
Jaspan, Norman, quoted, 115, 128
Jewish ghettos, 57
Johns, Veronica Parker, *44-46*
Johnson, Guy B., 58
Jones (Willwerth), 74-75
Judd, Winnie Ruth, *44-46*
Judges, 160-161
Juries, 157-160
Juvenile crime, 23-26, *52*; prostitution, *56-57*

K
Kalven, Harry, Jr., 157
Kelly, Kathryn, *44-46*
Kelly, "Machine Gun," 46
Kidnapping: Italy, 11, 14; Lindbergh, *28-39*
Klein, Alexander, quoted, 79
Kleptomania, 50
Knox, Robert, 17
Kobler, Arthur, 150
Kobler, John, *Capone*, 100
Koch, Ilse, 15
Kray, Charles, 85-86
Kray, Ronald and Reginald, *83*, 85-86

L
Labor unions, organized crime and, 96
Lacassagne, Jean, quoted, 55
LaGuardia, Fiorello, 102
Lang, Fritz, 61; *M, 66-67*
Lawton, Hughes, quoted, 120
Lebanon, 86
Ledda, Richard, 137
Lee, Manfred B., *44-46*
Lejeune, Jerome, 47-48
LIFE (magazine), *44-45*
Lindbergh, Anne, *29*
Lindbergh, Charles, *29*
Lindbergh kidnapping, *28-39*
Lindner, Robert, 52-53
Loan-sharking, 93-96
Lockheed Aircraft Corporation, 115, *130-131*, *132-134*
Lombroso, Cesare, *The Criminal Man*, 43-46; quoted, 43
London, 9, 10, *51*, 83; Chiswick Women's Aid Center, *20-21*; police, 142
Lonergan, Wayne, *44-46*
Loren, Sophia, 14
Lorre, Peter, *66-67*
Louisiana, organized crime in, 90
Luciano, Charles "Lucky," 84
Lyle, Walter, *34*
Lyons, John, *34*

M
M (film, Lang), *66-67*
Macbeth (Shakespeare), *62*

McCain, Alice, *152-155*
McCloy, Helen, *44-46*
McCully, E. Walbridge, *44-46*
McEwan, William, 42
Mack, John, 9-10; quoted, 9, 86
Madagascar, 155
Madis, Dr. Valdemar H., 120-121, 135
"Mafia," 26, 85, 87, 90, 96. *See also* Organized crime
Manchild in the Promised Land (Brown), 57
Manners, William, *44-46*
Mark, Sir Robert, quoted, 142
Marseilles, France, 85
Martinson, Robert, quoted, 164
Marubeni Corporation (Japan), 132
Masters, R. E. L., quoted, 80
Mastroianni, Marcello, *69*
Mattick, Hans, quoted, 164
Maurer, David, quoted, 72, 73, 78, 79
Mead, Margaret, 90
Medicare fraud, 118
Menninger, Karl, 51; quoted, 15, 39, 41, 50, 53
Mercy killing, 156
Merton, Robert, 57-58
Mesomorphs, 47
Mexico City, *16-17*
Michigan, organized crime in, 90
Miller, Walter, 41-42
Milner, Christina and Richard, 80-84
M'Naghten Rule, 157
Monsieur Verdoux (film, Chaplin), *64, 65*
Moran, Bugs, quoted, 105
More, Sir Thomas, 57
Mores, traditional, 58-59
Motor Vehicle Safety Act (1966), 133
Moyer, Kenneth, quoted, 48
Munich Olympics (1972), 141
Murder, 17-19; gangland executions, *88-89, 106-107*; rates, 42; sadistic, 55; suicide and, 51; trials for, 47-48, 49; "victim-precipitated homicides," 54; victims, *10-11*
Mussomeli, Sicily, *91*
Myers, Gustavus, quoted, 116-117
Mystery Novel Classics (magazine), 46
Mystery Writers of America, *44-45*, 46

N

Nader, Ralph, *133*
Naples, Italy, *52*
Netherlands, 86; Lockheed crisis, 115
Nevada, organized crime in, 90
New Guinea, Kai tribes, 153-154
New Jersey, organized crime in, 90
New York City, 23, *56-57*; organized crime, 7, 73, *88-89*; police, 139-142, *149, 152-155*; speak-easies, 22, *102-103*
New York *Daily News*, 28-29
New York State: organized crime, 90-92, 93;

Supreme Court (on Nixon), 115-118
New York Stock Exchange, 125
New York Times, The, *30-31*, 36
Newman, Donald, quoted, 153
Newspapers, and Lindbergh kidnapping, *28-39*
Nice, France, 114
Nixon, Richard M., 27, 115-118, 121
Norway, criminal-justice system, 157, 169
Numbers game, 92-93

O

O'Banion, Dion, *98-99*; St. Valentine's Day massacre, *104-105*
O'Connor, Charles, *152-153*
O'Donnell, Edward "Spike," *98-99*
Oedipus (Sophocles), *62-63*
Oedipus complex, 51, 53
Ohlin, Lloyd, quoted, 54-55
Oliver Twist (Dickens), 64
Olivier, Marie-Louise, 47
Organized crime, 84-97; Europe, 85-87; Japan, 27, 85; United States, 87-97
Ostrove, Nancy, 157-158
Othello (Shakespeare), *60-61*

P

Pakistani ghettos, 57
Paris, 9, 47; bank robbery, *74*; prostitution, 18
Parker, Bonnie, *81*
Peace, Charlie, 15
Peel, Sir Robert, 138
Penal colonies, *94-95*. *See also* Prisons
Petronius, 73
Philadelphia, Pennsylvania, 54, 57
Pickpockets, 7, *16-17*, 76, 78-79, 168
Pilferage, 96, 115, *118-119*
Pimps, 80-84. *See also* Prostitution
Plato, quoted, 168
Plea bargaining, 152-153
Police, 59, 138-150; arrests by, *136*, 148-150, *149, 152-155*; corruption, 97; and crime statistics, 8; and family quarrels, 139-141; and guns, 148-150; and hostages, 141-142; Interpol, 138-139; Japan, *143-146*; and television, *159*. *See also* Scotland Yard
"Police Five" (London TV program), 159
Political campaigns, organized crime and, 97
Pornography, 92
Portugal, death penalty, 163
Poverty, 23, *40*, 41, 57-58
Price-fixing, 115, 129-132; "electrical conspiracy," 124-128, 129
Prisons, 164-169; overcrowding, *162*; L'Asinara Island, *94-95*; Sing Sing, *127*, Sweden, *165-167*

Prohibition, 19-22, 87-90; Capone and, *98-111*
Property crimes, 17
Prosecution, 150-153
Prostitution, 47, 80-84, 92; blacks and, 57; France, *18*; teen-age runaways and, *56-57*
Psychological theories, 49-53
Punishment, 163-169; desire for, 51. *See also* Death sentence; Prisons

Q

Queen, Ellery, 46
Quiet Please, Murder (film, Blochman), 46

R

Racial discrimination, 57, 58
Radzinowicz, Sir Leon, quoted, 26
Redgrave, Michael, *62*
Reik, Theodor, quoted, 51
Rhode Island, organized crime in, 90
Rice University, 168
Richardson, Charles and Eddie, 85-86
Rime of the Ancient Mariner, The (Coleridge), *68, 69*
Robber barons, *116-117*, 129, 133
Robberies. *See* Bank robberies; Great Train Robbery (England, 1963); Theft
Robeson, Paul, *60-61*
Robson, Flora, *62*
Rossi, Christian, 151
Rothman, David, quoted, 164, 169
Rumrunners, *100*
Russier, Gabrielle, 151
Russo, Giuseppe Genco, *91*
Ryan, Pike, 73

S

Safecracking, *70*, 71-72
St. Valentine's Day massacre (1929), *104-105*
Sakata, Genichiro, 85
Saltis, Joe, *98-99*
San Jose, California, 118
Sanders, Joseph, quoted, 158, 160
Sawyer, Peter Roland (Tom), quoted, 149-150
Scandinavia, 163. *See also* Norway; Sweden
Schlossberg, Harvey, quoted, 141
Schur, Edwin, quoted, 26, 79, 135
Schwimmer, Reinhardt, 105
Scotland, 10
Scotland Yard, 138, 139
Seattle, Washington, 115
Seitz, Sepp, *152-155*
Sellin, Thorsten, 168
Seneca, 17
Sentencing. *See* Punishment
Sergovich, Fred, quoted, 48
Severin, Kurt, *44-46*
Sex, and crime, 50-51, 52-53. *See also* Prostitution

174

Shady Doings (Johns), 46
Shakespeare, William, 14, 61; *Macbeth, 62; Othello, 60-61*
Shaw, Donald, 97
Shaw, George Bernard, *The Crime of Imprisonment*, 164
Sheldon, William, 47
Sherman Antitrust Act (1890), 124
Shinnar, Shlomo and Reuel, 169
Shoplifting, 11, 50, *140, 149*; professional (boosters), 76-78
Sicily, *82-83*, 90, *91*, 92, *94-95*
Sigall, Harold, 157-158
Sing Sing Prison, *127*
Singing Widow, The (Johns), 46
Slums. *See* Poverty
Smith (amateur shoplifter), 76
Smith, Charles, quoted, 160
Smuggling, *86*, 87
Sociological theories, 52, 53-59 56-57, 64-65
Solomon, George, 51
Sophocles, 61; *Oedipus, 62-63*
South Carolina, prison camp, *162*
Southern Pacific Railroad, *116-117*
Soviet Union, 8, 11, 19; courts, 156; white-collar crime, 134-135
Spain, 86; Basque terrorists, *24-25*; juries, 157
Sparta (ancient), 17
Speak-easies, 22, *102-103*
Speck, Richard, 48-49
Spencer, John, 128
Stainbrook, Edward, 168-169; quoted, 169
Stanford, Leland, *116-117*
Steele, Floyd, 142
Stenson, Joseph, 100
Stephen, Sir James, quoted, 163-164
"Stigmata," 43
Stranger, The (Camus), *69*
Streetwalking. *See* Prostitution
Suicide, and murder, 51
Sumeria, 164
Sutherland, Edwin H., 54, 113
Sutton, Willie, 81, *82*
Sweden, 86; prisons, 164-168, *165-167*
Swindlers. *See* Confidence men
Switzerland, criminal-justice system, 157, 163

Sydney *Daily Telegraph*, 15
"Syndicate, The," 87. *See also* Organized crime

T
Tax fraud, 11, 114
Teen-age runaways, *56-57*. *See also* Juvenile crime
Television, police and, *159*
Teresa, Charles, quoted, 96
Terrorism, 141; Basque, *24-25*; German, 9-10. *See also* Hostages
Theft, 19; organized crime and, 86-87, 96. *See also* Bank robberies; Great Train Robbery (England, 1963)
Titteron, Nancy, 46
To Die of Love (film), 151
Togo, 154
Tokyo Police Academy, *143-145*
Torrio, Johnny, *44-46*
Touhy gang (Chicago), 46
Treat, Lawrence, *44-46*
Triads (Hong Kong), 85
Trial by ordeal, 154-155
Tullio, Benigno di, 58
Turkey, 86; drug smuggling, *87*
Turpin, Dick, 15
Tyler, Gus, quoted, 87, 93-96

U
Uganda, Entebbe airport rescue (1976), 142
Union Corse (Europe), 85
United Nations, 114, 148
U.S. antitrust laws, 124-128, 129
U.S. Chamber of Commerce, 114
U.S. Coast Guard, *100*
U.S. Constitution, 157
U.S. Supreme Court, and abortion, 22
University of Houston, 168
University of London, 26
University of Louisville, 72
University of Maryland, 158
University of Michigan, 158
University of Pennsylvania, 23, 163
University of Washington, 160
"Upperworld" crime, 57
Ur-Nammu, King (Sumeria), 164

V
V as in Victim (Treat), 46
Van den Haag, Ernest, quoted, 57
Van Meegeren, Hans, 17
Vanderbilt, Cornelius, 129; quoted, 116-117
Vanderbilt, William H., *116-117*
Victimless crimes, 17, 19-23
"Victim-precipitated homicides," 54
Victims: murder, *10-11*; wife-beating, *20-21*
Vilella (criminal), 43
Violence, 9, 55, 59
Violencia (Colombia), 55

W
Wales, 10
Walpole, Horace, quoted, 7
Washburn, Sherwood L., quoted, 47
Watergate affair, 115-118
Webb, Clifton, 36
Webster, Daniel, quoted, 114
Weil, Joseph ("Yellow Kid"), *44-46*, 79
West Berlin, 10
West Germany, 9-10, 11, 14, 86; criminal-justice system, 156, 163; television, *159*
Wheeler, Stanton, 59
Whitney, Richard, *125-127*
Whittaker, Ben, quoted, 150
Wholesome Meat Act (1967), 133
Whyos gang (New York City), 73
Wife-beating, *20-21*
William Brown (U.S. ship), 156
Willwerth, James, *Jones*, 74-75
Wilson, Frank J., 111
Wilson, Herbert Emerson, 71-72
Wine frauds (France and Italy), 118-120, *122*
Wolfgang, Marvin, 23-26, 163, 169; quoted, 53-54, 55
Women, and crime, 26
World War II, 26

Y
Yamaguchi, Harukichi, 27
"Yellow Kid" (Joseph Weil), *44-46*, 79
Yugoslavia, 86

Z
Zeisel, Hans, 157
Ziporyn, Marvin, 48-49

Printed in U.S.A.